D1062421

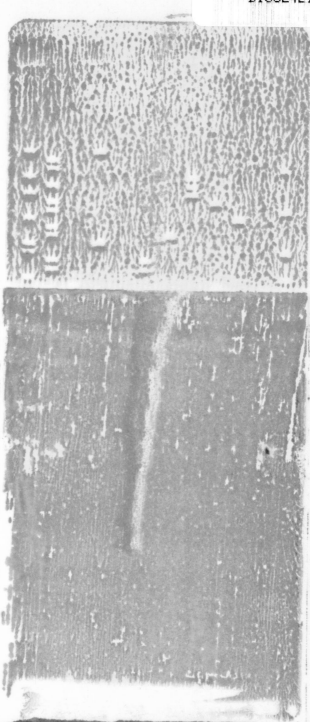

# GENERAL WILLIAM GROENER

# AND THE

# IMPERIAL GERMAN ARMY

by

Helmut Haeussler

*THE STATE HISTORICAL SOCIETY OF WISCONSIN*
*for*
*THE DEPARTMENT OF HISTORY, UNIVERSITY OF WISCONSIN*
*Madison, 1962*

# 1980726

PRINTED IN THE UNITED STATES OF AMERICA BY

BOOK CRAFTSMEN ASSOCIATES, INC., NEW YORK

# CONTENTS

## DEDICATION AND ACKNOWLEDGMENTS

This book is dedicated to my father and mother, who shared in the life of the Second German Empire and reflected its virtues. It is written as an outgrowth of a study begun under the careful hand of Professor Chester V. Easum of the University of Wisconsin. He first directed me into the Groener materials, and he has been mentor and consultant in the progress of this work.

I wish also to express my appreciation to Professor Theodore Hamerow and the publication committee of the Department of History for providing this opportunity to present Groener's Empire career in book form. A special debt of gratitude is due the editorial staff of the publisher for their resilient patience with my manuscript problems.

Certain requirements of format have forced me to concentrate the Groener story and supply only representative notes.

Helmut Haeussler

California Lutheran College
October, 1961

# INTRODUCTION

History knows William Groener mostly for three significant deeds. He directed the railroad mobilization in 1914 which launched the German strike into Belgium and northern France. He managed the German army in its hour of defeat and guided its difficult alignment with the Weimar republic. Finally, he shared in the Bruening cabinet's losing effort to sustain that state in its terminal agonies with economic depression and political dissension. Groener's generation inherited the assumptions of a powerful Empire and was forced to absorb the shock of military defeat and ideological change. The dignity of earlier years gave way to the helplessness of the Weimar experience and the disgrace of Nazi abandon.

Groener played a conspicuous role in the life of his time and his nation's tragedy encompassed his own sense of frustration and disillusionment. As a dedicated soldier and disciple of Schlieffen, he was to be estranged from his General Staff colleagues because of his part in the Imperial collapse and the republican experiment. He was the first to tell Kaiser William II that the Hohenzollern command of the army was finished and he espoused the Weimer republic as the best emergency vehicle of continuing national interest. As one who had himself dreamed of a century of German dominance in Europe, he was to be scorned by later critics of defeat as a soldier who had resisted the command of his superior and pacted with a revolutionary republic. Himself a monarchist, he was a greater nationalist and he chose to salvage German unity in November, 1918, rather than invite disintegrating civil war by continuing military support of

vii

Kaiser William's authority.   He understood that an entire
people could not be asked to commit suicide for the sake of
a failing dynasty.

Groener's effort to help direct a reasonable German reaction to the realities of defeat epitomized the psychic dilemma of the Weimar state.  Men who looked back on the Empire
as the finer world were confronted with new conditions of
national life.  Groener and his friends regarded the new democracy as a destiny, not an ideal, but they stood up to the
disheartening turn of events and served the Weimar society
as best they could.  Communist dangers were brought under
control and even the patriotic Social Democrats were gradually
brought into more conservative bourgeois harness.  Such compromise republicanism was little appreciated by either the
left or right wings of German political feeling, and the Staatsraeson of Groener and others could not muster consistent
public resonance.  It was easier to condemn and promise more
decisively, and all too often those who lost the war pointed
accusing fingers at those who had assumed the responsibilities
of defeat.  Under the republic the chauvinist critics dominated
only the printed page, but they shared in the Nazi triumph and
thereafter enjoyed official sanction.  Groener and his fellow
Weimar leaders were swept aside and he lived out his last
few years in the shadows of general disfavor.

Groener wrote his memoirs in the late nineteen thirties
but they were somewhat controversial for the day and publication was then postponed by the outbreak of World War II.  His
papers were shipped into the quiet repose of the Heeresarchiv.
They were subsequently taken to America and finally returned
to Germany in 1955.   In microfilm form, they consist of
twenty-seven rolls of book drafts, articles, memoranda, correspondence, war journals, War Academy notes, day books,
army problems, speeches and newspaper clippings.  Hiller von
Gaertringen's introduction to the Groener autobiography, published in 1957, described some of the source material and
generally recognized its value and reliability.  The alterations
which Groener effected in his various autobiographic drafts
and even in some of his letters do not weaken the substantial
reliability of his material.   The abundance of raw sources
makes critical view and evaluation readily possible.

Groener's material does much to mark the limitations

of his biography by daughter Dorothea Groener-Geyer. Her source foundation was rather narrow and the story was, understandably enough, in the nature of an _apologia_. She did align much of the Weimar material and make it available to a broader audience. But she tended to disregard the earlier militarism of her father and stress only his more judicious _Staatsraeson_ after 1917. The general's own autobiography then pointed out his wartime transformation from militaristic naivete to broader political circumspection giving real evolutionary depth and development to his life. Now origins and change were visible, rather than mere Weimar maturity.

Groener's papers and person are thus in some distinct outline, although continuing clarification and processing is only in a beginning state. There is no full length, or critically objective, biography. Much of his material still merits editing and publication. His view of state and army in the variable Weimar republic has not really been worked out, and the interesting themes of his military career have not been adequately identified and delineated. His dramatic exchange with dynastic interests at Spa on November 9 was only the climatic moment of earlier breeding, experience, and deliberation. Such an analysis of his imperial life and career, as it leads up to November, 1918, is the subject of our study. Its form and material cannot claim exhaustive or definitive presentation but improved knowledge and comprehension of Groener's life should be made possible. And it may help to focus this story if certain other aspects of his Empire role are also given advance mention at this time.

Groener represented the entry of the bourgeois technical soldier onto the German war scene. He was one of the first to understand the vital significance of machines and factories in twentieth century war. His General Staff work plunged him into railroad transportation detail usually shunned by the more influential or fanciful. He became a key architect of the western mobilization and he learned to master the function of rail transportation in modern mass strategy. The Schlieffen Plan relied on speed and Groener's mobilization in 1914 unfolded with superb precision. Then, as trench war ensued, his railroads swung between east and west to implement every dangerous German pivotal action for the remainder of the war.

Groener's railroad _desiderata_ were frequently slighted

by the commanding strategists and he lamented often that they did not fully understand the key role of transportation to modern mass strategy.  His grasp of technical war was then deepened by a ten-month tour of duty in Berlin as Germany's first chief of an economic War Office.  From February until October, 1918, he managed German operations in Ukraine, where Ludendorff expected him to turn crumbs into food trains. Groener knew first-hand about wartime labor and politics in Berlin and he was intimate with the problems of the Russian Revolution in Kiev.  In fact, such rear echelon experience pushed him into his fatal liquidation assignment on the western front in November, 1918.  He was picked to replace Ludendorff because he could best organize a German withdrawal or demobilization.  Since he had earlier gained the confidence of the Social Democrats in Berlin, he seemed best equipped to represent the army amid the democratic changes which could no longer be avoided in the Fall of   1918. Groener's technical talent had led him into home front industrial assignments which gave him the political and labor contacts so vital to the interests of army and emperor in the crisis weeks of October and November, 1918.

Groener was a modern German nationalist.  He was a Swabian of modest family circumstance who was excited by the expanded prestige and opportunity which the new Empire offered.  This son of a frustrated warrant officer in the army of Wuerttemberg climbed eagerly upwards in the more capacious structure and higher status of the Empire army.  It was still controlled by the Prussian aristocrat, but its very growth into a modern mass force brought into it more and more bourgeois and proletariat elements. Expansive national interests had to be asserted by expanded national armies and German particularism was giving ground before such comradeship of arms.  Alert young bourgeois sons like Groener were needed and they would bring a new German patriotism into the Hohenzollern army.  His sort regarded the Empire army as a national, not a dynastic institution, and they understood it as an arm of the German, not royal interest.  Prussian possessiveness in things military might be respected only as long as it correlated with effective and progressive national service. And the Empire army was fairly successful in blending vested junker interests with new bourgeois ambitions and with new national objectives. General patriotic ego and economic interests were well pleased with German power, and Prussian military leadership appeared capable of serving the nation and amalgamating with broader circles of the citizenry.

The General Staff had room for such bourgeois types as Groener, Kuhl, and Hoffman even though they were yet assigned the less exciting chores. Their technical chores unwittingly established them as the critical experts in the mechanical and industrial warfare which developed after the opening Marne campaign in 1914. Groener felt himself to be at home in the General Staff and he tended to look on vestiges of Prussian exclusiveness as innocuous mementos of the past. He never shared the class consciousness of his many aristocratic colleagues but he respected their mettle and regarded them as his comrades. He was no advocate of parliamentary government either, but he did not feel himself to be threatened by politicians, merchants, or workers. They were fellow citizens of different viewpoint who also had their rightful place and voice in the new Empire. Groener even wrote an article before the war in which he advocated the army as a unifying experience and training school for the entire German citizenry.

A new national spirit, surmounting past class and regional prejudice, was to be forged amid the comradeship of arms. Such an integration of spirit was both realized and lost in the course of World War I. The unity of 1914 gradually gave way to renewed class suspicions and alienation as victory hopes began to fade despite the colossal sacrifices of total war. The crisis of the war posed the question of the nation's survival and future, and it probed social and political feeling to the bone. In 1918, Groener would place national continuity above dynastic ego and be resented by many a comrade who held his oath of personal fealty to the Kaiser to be most sacred. German hierarchies were not yet integrated and worlds of past and modern loyalties were here divided. Most German leaders, regardless of their choice, were deeply wrenched by the loss of their old world and they were heartsick in the new state. This was the psychic problem of the Weimar republic and it too burdened Groener's heart, for he had made such a painful personal decision in choosing national continuity over Kaiser William II.

The development of Groener's national spirit from militant enthusiasm to calculating _Staatsraeson_ was a most interesting facet of his ideological growth. _Staatsraeson_ may be described in short as the ethical and rational implementation of state power. Not nullifying the opportunities of strength, it calls for the politics of the possible, and seeks to maintain in all political life a restraining sense of civility and moderation. Groener was rather devoid of such political ethic during the early years of the war when he thought mostly of complete victory and a century of German dominance in Europe. He disregarded more complex considerations of state as he urged the full use of the Schlieffen Plan despite    ominous diplomatic implications. He and his friends thought to recoup the fading German fortune on the battlefield and they were willing to resolve all issues militarily. Even after the Marne, the will to win still possessed Groener and he was angrily resentful of any talk about a "lazy peace." Then as German strength began to wilt in 1916, he began to understand those who argued for timely negotiation. He had contact with such men as Hans Delbrueck and Friedrich Meinecke, and perhaps their more comprehensive considerations helped him to change from a "naive" to a political soldier. By 1917 he was in favor of diplomatic negotiation and domestic reform.

The Empire needed rest and modern reorganization if it expected to continue a role of international influence in the years to come. Now Groener understood that national policy had deeper determinants than momentary battlefield _desiderata_. The army should henceforth obediently screen for the diplomatic rescue rather than exercise a simple will to win. Such timely flexibility was not effected as the Empire leaders chose to dare a victory peace instead. And they got it at Compiegne and Versailles. By then Groener was in a position of influence but his choice remained only between national surrender or suicide. For very instinctive reasons of state, the German choice was elementary and rationally unavoidable. Under the Weimar republic Groener would try to rebuild a foundation of German strength and carefully recover a degree of international security and maneuverability. Groener would cherish the dream of a Schlieffen victory to his dying day, but after 1917 such military fancies were carefully curbed by broader and more cautious political consideration.

Groener's political wisdom emerged only as victory slipped out of reach and it need not be lauded as a remarkable accomplishment.  Many other Germans arrived at similar conclusions in a not too difficult exercise of reason.  But Groener was one of the few soldiers who had the courage to speak up and it was here that he played a lonely role.  For it he was stigmatized even before 1918, and his renunciation of the Kaiser's authority at Spa only gave historic climax to his reorientation.  National continuity itself seemed to be at stake in those final weeks in October and November, 1918.  The military operation was admittedly lost and the Kaiser fled from angry reform repercussions in Berlin to his military headquarters at Spa.

Fears of a Russian-style revolution were acute and Groener's months in Kiev made him doubly afraid of such political chaos with its resultant national disintegration.  Then talk of Bavaria's withdrawal from Hohenzollern Germany became rife, and at Spa the Kaiser asked for counter-revolutionary action and talked about going home at the head of his own Prussian troops.  A national break-up loomed ahead and it was in such a moment of crisis, on November 9, that a fearful and exasperated Groener finally told the Kaiser that "the army will march home in peace and order under its leaders and commanding generals, but not under the command of Your Majesty, for it no longer stands behind Your Majesty."  These were fatal words, spoken in the Hohenzollern's military camp even as Berlin mobs overthrew his authority at home.

Groener's dramatic statement at Spa voiced the thought of Hindenburg and it rested on a poll of almost half a hundred frontline commanders.  One might even see here a beginning of that dilemma of command and obedience which attained fuller scope in World War II.  It seems permissible and necessary to say that Groener expressed a consensus military view at Spa even though royalist sympathizers and bitter critics would later portray his action in terms of a disobedient coup.  There heroes at the Spa meeting, such as Schulenburg and the Crown Prince, could only argue that they still had the troops "firmly in hand."  These were paltry and archaic words after four years of colossal sacrifice as the fate of the nation itself hung in the balance.  It was a claim without modern sense or ethic, belied by evident facts and even by their own

complaints about rear echelon disorder and home front dissension. The soldiers who later resisted Hitler were confronted by a much more fundamental ethical problem. But
perhaps even Groener's demonstration of civic responsibility
can be understood as a beginning, or perhaps renewal, of the
German soldier's will to respect limits in command.

Groener learned that modern military power depended
on technical resources and mass psychological commitment.
National policy could not disregard geo-political capacities;
democratic feeling and continental limitations were impera-
tives to successful German policies of the future. Groener
learned that his army could not dominate Europe and that it
should not direct the larger national strategy. His hope that
the Empire might make its own timely adjustment was negated.
Then he sought to awaken in the Weimar army a willingness
to serve the republic and he asked postwar Germany to accept
a more modest future in European affairs. At best, it might
someday recover a position of continental influence, but only
by way of quiet economic energy and cautious diplomatic recovery. Such curtailment of his power ego was not easy and
his nation pulled away to follow the more impulsive program
of National Socialism.

Now, in mid-century, it seems that the Staatsraeson
of Groener, Meinecke and company has found a broader base
of popular support and international friendship. The German
power ego is apparently adjusted to its limitations and to
Europe's associative needs. Now it is Europe which must itself learn new modesties in its international life. In the
broader German and European context, Groener's lesson in
the restraint and ethic of power represents a timely and universal political experience.

Chapter One

FORMATIVE YEARS

William Groener was born on November 22, 1867, in
the southern German kingdom of Wuerttemberg. The Swabian
background undoubtedly prepared him for later republican adjustments and a glimpse into his Wuerttemberg life is a logical first step in our effort to understand his person.

Certainly the Swabians did not excel in state growth,
as did the Prussians. They were content with a modest position in Germany's various confederate systems and they
directed their political attention more toward internal refinement. In past centuries they had chased out more than one
ruler and executed more than one minister of state. One notable eighteenth century British statesman once commented that
in Europe only Britain and Wuerttemberg had constitutions
worthy of the name. The Swabians retained many of the liberal institutions introduced by Napoleon and, with the men
of Baden, they led in the progressive resistance against
Metternich's Restoration restrictions. The southwest liberals
and republicans gave key strength to left-wing sentiment in
the Frankfurt Parliament in 1848 and it was a Swabian delegate, poet Ludwig Uhland, who there coined the celebrated
phrase that the German crown should be anointed "with a drop
of democratic oil." And he swore to "no one single man," for
one he was himself.

The Parliament of 1848-1849 made its last stand in
Stuttgart as the rump group moved to this democratic strong-
hold after the Frankfurt session dissolved. And in the momentary flash of rebellious confusion which accompanied the
final defeat of the revolution, the officers of the Wuerttem-

1

berg army told their King that his rights were measured by the
Frankfurt and Wuerttemberg constitutions. As citizens and
as soldiers, they did not believe him to have unconditional
authority.

After the revolution Prussia and Austria began a final
duel for the controlling position in Germany. The northern
kingdom veered toward a policy of hegemony interest and
consolidation. The Danube empire hoped to continue a multi-
state Germany in which it could further forestall any Prussian
union. The small states sought to evade this power rivalry
if possible but they were finally forced into a decisive choice.
In 1866 most of the small state governments entered into the
German civil war on the side of Austria, since the Hapsburg
program promised to sustain, rather than integrate, German
federalism.

Wuerttemberg's diplomatic maneuvers in these final
years of Prussian-Austrian rivalry typified small-state apprehension and flexibility. Certainly its citizens had need of
a sense of pessimistic Realpolitik in order to understand the
frequent diplomatic switching and disappointments. Wuerttemberg stayed neutral with Prussia in the Crimean War, to
the irritation of both France and Russia. It favored Austria
against France in 1859, and Napoleon won. It supported the
Prince of Augustenberg's claim to Schleswig-Holstein, but
Austria and Prussia shared mandate rights over the two penin-
sular provinces after their detachment from Denmark. A perplexed Wuerttemberg court then dared the decisive step in
1866 and joined Austria in the war against Prussia.

The behavior of the Wuerttembergers in that war of
1866 was rather typical of small-state opportunism and realism. At the outset of conflict, Foreign Minister Varnbueler
cried vae victis to the Prussians, and his fellow citizens
talked cockily of marching into Brandenburg. When Prussian
power revealed itself, all such ebullience disappeared quickly. Within a month, as the story goes, the same Varnbueler
found himself sitting on a beer keg outside Bismarck's tent
in Bohemia, waiting to receive terms. As one of the home
patriots wrote to Varnbueler: "It is yet possible to save our
fine land and our brave soldiers from the fate of needless
sacrifice." Desperate heroism seemed entirely senseless to
these junior partners in German politics and spirited beginning

notwithstanding, Wuerttemberg had enough realistic sense
of self-preservation to jump off the war chariot once the ride
became both pointless and suicidal. The Varnbueler anecdote
is not without humor and it may have real meaning for the
Swabian philosophy of war and politics. Interestingly enough,
Groener received the same sort of letter from a Swabian
countryman in November, 1918, as did Varnbueler at the
point of defeat.    War was senseless when victory was no
longer possible and when it must lead only to greater loss of
life and the ruination of the homeland.[1]

Swabian enthusiasm was deeper and more lasting in
the unification war with France. The interest of the Southwest in a national state was finally rewarded and those Germans were wholeheartedly happy even though Prussian leadership meant a less liberal constitution than they might have
wanted.    But a covering national form was now reality,
Swabian autonomies were respected and future constitutional
improvements could be effected in the years to come.    The
Swabian military were especially happy with the new developments.    In the words of Schlieffen, as he observed them
during the Franco-Prussian war, "They are imbued with a
genuine enthusiasm for Prussia and admire features of ours
which do not even impress us. Furthermore, all these
Wuerttemberg officers are charming and sociable."[2]    They
were happy to climb aboard an organization of European range
and fame and their careers suddenly had magnified scope.
Generally a step below the social level of their new aristocratic Prussian colleages, they had the ease and ego of
personality to disregard class differences and assume the
human contact. Of course such differences were not thereby
eliminated and their relationship would retain its paradoxical
nature.

The Swabians were rooted in looser democratic soil
and they did not have the class pride and mannerism of the
Prussian aristocrat, but they could respect the industry and
integrity of the latter and admire the scope of his activity.
The new identification with great power interests titillated
the erstwhile small-staters and they venerated Bismarck and
Moltke as German patriots, if not as Prussian aristocrats.
As yet the new Empire lacked constitutional symmetry or even
full spiritual unity, but it was a living thing, capable of

self-development and self-defense, and it remained to be
seen how well this Empire and its army could fuse conglom-
erate tensions into strong and binding unity.

Groener's father was a frustrated paymaster in the
Wuerttemberg army, born too soon for the Empire opportunities. His orbit was narrowly fixed and he chafed at the
thought that his talents never had a chance for full bloom.
His son, William, could and did stretch for a bigger place
in the sun and he recognized that such expanded opportunity
was made possible by the new national life. From his father's
family he inherited the tenacity, frankness, and occasional
brusqueness common to the natives of the picturesque hill
and dale Swabian Alb. His mother stemmed from a bourgeois
family which had travelled a road of patient, ambitious progress. It had a meticulous trait which was probably passed
on to the future railroad general. Young William spent some
years in the old free city of Ulm with its smug,   self-conscious
burgher atmosphere. Its time-honored garrison soldiers were
welcome intimates but also tolerated guests and the Swabian
military in no sense dominated their society. The spirit ap-
proximated that of a militia setting, though the organization
might be professional. Groener matured in these small cities
of Wuerttemberg where social life was substantially informal
and where no one group could seriously elevate itself above
the other.

Groener's memoirs also gave a special place of importance to the hiking trips of his youth. These were practically an institution in nineteenth century Wuerttemberg.   Rich
and poor streamed out into nature,  shared the same excursion
paths and sought refreshment and conviviality in the same
inn.   And its long benches and tables defied segregation.
There the public rubbed elbows with itself, discussed politics and cheered up the day with a good glass of beer. Here
was a style of life, informal, hearty, intimate and unconsciously democratic.   Political and class differences in
Wuerttemberg were not stiff and hostile.   There was social
exchange among the people and between factions.   People
were accustomed to political disagreement not exaggerated
into a life and death struggle of tradition, honor, or even
interest. The King visited his legislature. Social Democrats
were not considered to be dangerous pariahs and they in turn

respected their state, even in opposition. The soldiers as-
sociated with the civilians and they were not elevated behind
special walls of privilege. Groener's memory of his earlier
years was perhaps not free of romanticism and yet there evi-
dently was a social lubricant which gave basic human equality and cohesion to Swabian society. Groener was never
estranged by the common man and he maintained such egalitarian social forms throughout his life.

In 1884 Groener took a trip to Berlin to take a qualifying examination for entrance into a Prussian officer's candi-
date school. Then, on his seventeenth birthday, he enlisted
in the Wuerttemberg army. The young man wanted to relieve
the family budget and begin his own independence. He had
grown up in a barrack setting and he was alert to the opportunities in the new German army. Where else could one of
his simple background find a chance to develop a career in
which security, prestige, even democratic opportunity was
so capaciously available? Moltke's army was generally accepted as the first institution of the land and Groener stepped
into it with pride and ambition. He began his basic training
in Ludwigsburg and even participated in the Fall maneuvers
of 1884 where he saw Moltke, William I, and the future William II. The epic men and traditions of the unification army
were still present and the young soldier who would later become known as the Liquidation General worked happily into
a promising career. His qualifying scores soon came through
from Berlin and early in 1885 he moved up to an officer training academy near Coblenz.

The two years along the middle Rhine saw care-free
fledgling growth and careful professional training. There he
and other young military enthusiasts were introduced to the
duties of army life and to the art of war. The Academy commander was wise enough to close an eye now and then, and
the spirit of his young cadets was directed, rather than com-
pressed. Groener was impressed by this relaxed rein and he
apparently developed comparable tact and human understanding in his own leadership. Down through the years he would
be an officer who granted autonomy and expected precision.
His Academy work showed a distinct flair for the practical.
He was only "satisfactory" in drill, fencing and mount knowledge, but he was "good" in riding, gymnastics and marks-

manship. His bearing was "outstanding" and his superiors
noted freshness and originality in his work. He did excel in
military history and here practical troop command was enhanced by academic talent. Groener finally returned to his
home unit in 1886 with a lieutenant's commission and an ele-
vating future well in sight. [3]

Not yet twenty, the young officer then lapsed into the
easy hum-drum of the peacetime army. His regiment had only
recently participated in an Imperial maneuver and such Fall
excitement was not liable to return too soon. Groener drilled
and lectured his men, trained the squad and maneuvered the
platoon. The work was routine and he slid lazily into tavern
pastimes. He and his colleagues had their morning and evening drinks, and Groener did the town with enough persistence
to be finally dubbed the "night light." He was usually the
last man home. At their inns the young officers exchanged
boisterous comradeship and sang sarcastic songs about the
civilians. In the later night hours it was not unusual for them
to improvise a parade ground by sliding the tables together.
On such a stage they would demonstrate their parade step and
gradually the inspectors would pull the tables apart until
some bold-striding warrior fell short and down. Such antics
were harmless enough although the entire army apparently
was beset by such boredom and gambling and drinking were
becoming real problems.

The Groener group had their jokes about civilians but
their laughs and songs hardly expressed caste feeling. The
bachelor officers ate in the public inns with the regular
burgher clientele and an egalitarian social atmosphere prevailed. Yet certain changes were also coming into vogue
during these very years. Some of the officer groups in Wuerttemberg were beginning to reserve separate dining rooms and
in 1893 the new King, trained in Prussia, inaugurated the
first officer's club, or "Kasino", in Ludwigsburg. Bourgeois
officers were seeping into the Prussian caste structure but at
the same time certain junker military features were also
reaching into the non-Prussian lands.

In Prussia the Kasino represented the secluded retreat
and citadel of the military caste. There the officers could
eat, read, play and drink among their own kind. It was not
merely a convenient place of assembly for military friends,

but it was dedicated to the maintenance of a separate military society. The Kasino consciously sought to preserve the "officer's corps from the disintegrating influences" of an outside world growing ever more strange and hostile. In the Kasino the old guard could "keep a watchful eye over the younger members" and protect the traditional spirit. The breach between the military and the civilian worlds was publicly recognized in Prussia where the officer's corps actively pursued its factional interest by building rest homes, creating trust funds, publishing newspapers, and applying political leverage wherever they could.

Modern methods of factional self-assertion were employed in order to defend established privileges. They had their own honor courts for delinquents and one Prussian noble was temporarily stripped of rank and decorations for voting with reform elements in the Reichstag. That representative assembly was generally unhappy with the class and caste implications of the Kasino, especially since such club costs drew from the regular army budget. But the Reichstag could not penetrate the constitutional autonomy of the army in its administrative, and even fiscal, matters. Old Moltke could stand up among his fellow legislators and concede that they might determine the periodic sum for military expenditures, but that they had no right to control specific items within that budget. He quietly told the anti-military critics that "we have another word for caste spirit; we call it comradeship." To bourgeois ears these were specious words although the old man probably meant them in all positive sincerity. The exclusive, hierarchic traditions of a passing world were simply out of step with the march for new mass equality and mass authority.[4]

The Kasinos were moving south and the democrats were going north, to the Reichstag in Berlin. The parts and people of the new Empire were beginning to engage and a new body politic was being formed. The Empire grew up with the industrial revolution and the privileged leadership of the founding fathers was almost immediately challenged by an industrializing society. The patrimonial style of the Hohenzollern regime could not dignify the will and self-respect of the modern masses who demanded equal rights for vital labor. But determined and militant junker stubbornness frankly blocked

constitutional improvement and consciously discounted any
deeper cohesion of the Empire spirit.  They believed in hierarchic alignment and trusting obedience, not general equality
and collective self-determination.  Thus the leadership and
the sustaining energy of Empire growth were in almost immediate tension against one another and this new society's para-
moun  problem was one of domestic integration.  But Bismarck
tried to repress mass rights and the repelled socialists responded with comparable hardness and enmity.  Liberal compromise efforts between these two poles of political force
were abused by the right and spurned by the left.

By 1890 the government and people of this great power
were still spiritually separated from one another even though
its outward force and inward order were unquestionable.
Junker dominance in the army and the bureaucracy represented
vital positions of control for that class, in coalition with the
Kaiser who staffed the national ministry, made war and peace
and absolutely controlled the armed force.  Democratic opposition centered in the Reichstag where criticism of suffrage
discrimination and junker immunities was consistent and bitter.  But incumbent conservative control was protected by
constitutional decrees and unwittingly assisted by the radical
revolutionary program of early German socialism which drove
the bourgeois parties toward the right.  Frequent diplomatic
dangers also tended to rally the people around their government and make criticism of the army consistently unpopular.
Bismarck, Moltke, and their successors would repeatedly
disarm a suspicious Reichstag with warnings of military danger and appeals for comradeship in arms.  Yet it was also
persistently evident that the Prussian leaders did not represent
German sentiment and that theirs was a selfish, outmoded
concept of political authority.

Groener was a satisfied monarchist officer and the socialists had nothing to say to him, but he got a taste of the
Empire's ideological frictions even in the more peaceful and
homogeneous Wuerttemberg.  The Kaiser gave up his brief effort to conciliate labor and by 1891 they were again portrayed
as national traitors.  William even told his Guards that they
must be prepared to shoot their own fathers and brothers;
chivalry apparently excluded the ladies. [5]  Feeling was not
that savage down in Wuerttemberg, but even Groener's unit

had its first May Day alert in 1891 and there were frequent
searches in the garrison for subversive literature. Once the
commander answered an anti-militaristic editorial by marching the regiment, band and all, past the windows of the in-
solent press. Such ideological skirmishing occurred throughout the Empire and it served to develop a deep rift of antag-
onism and suspicion between the military and the political
proletariat. This class breach was momentarily sealed by the
great crisis reconciliation in 1914, but it would open again
during the course of the war and plague the Empire with its
unresolved internal discriminations and tensions.

Groener's career did not get lost in such petty doctrinal
police work. He found himself drawn toward strategic studies
and by 1892 he was immersed in preparation for the qualifying examinations to the War Academy. Competition was sharp
and only about 20 per cent of the candidates were usually
accepted, but the erstwhile "night light" shifted successfully
to the midnight oil and in 1893 he made another big jump upwards. The paymaster's son was accepted into the Prussian
War Academy and both of the Groener men had a high sense
of family satisfaction. The Imperial army was still very much
an aristocratic institution, but more and more young Germans
like Groener were being fitted into the Prussian military machinery. Their talent and vital usefulness were unquestionable but it remained to be seen whether their social attitudes
would receive, or infiltrate, the Prussian tradition.

Groener's Swabian heritage came from a state which
had genuine concepts of charter rights and royal limitations.
His people felt and practiced a social egalitarianism which
softened class difference, lubricated political exchange, and
tempered authority all along the line. Men like Uhland did
not swear to "a single man" and the Wuerttemberg military
placed the constitution above the King. Wuerttemberg's struggle to survive in confederate Germany, especially in the climactic 60's, induced a Realpolitik of agile adjustment and
the example of Varnbueler seems aptly symbolic.

Groener's personality was composite even before he
moved into the Prussian stage of his development. He had
burgher blood and a garrison childhood. He became an officer
under Prussian training but he served his practical appren-
ticeship in Wuerttemberg's small cities, which were virtual

citadels of bourgeois life. He knew that world and its people and he also understood that proletariat programs could not simply be outlawed; they also represented social right and will. The twenty-five year old Groener's rootspread was not narrow and he was ready for an even bigger world. The Prussian War Academy would certainly add new features and dimensions to his growth,  possibly even lead him into the higher army circles. As yet his class limits were not visible and his national patriotism was not vexed by particularistic intransigence.  The new Germany offered a seemingly clear road to his ambitions and Groener went to Berlin with high confidence in his future.

The old capital of the Mark was now the forum of Germany,  the political focal point of Europe and a leading city of the world.  Here diplomats engaged in global enterprise while generals wondered desperately how to solve continental assignments.  The Empire's energy and ambition simply disregarded the modest or the cautious. A staid bureaucracy and an infant navy were hurried to overseas positions even though ill-prepared to manage global fronts.  There were constitutional problems enough at home and some wondered whether the new Empire was settled enough internally to venture on rather immediate global expansion. But a dramatic young Kaiser got on the bridge in 1888 and would show his subjects how to steer a world course, with full steam.  His policy was not mere personal whim for a very substantial body of economic and patriotic interest also insisted on world activity.  Even the workers could be brought to believe that colonies spelled industrial prosperity for both high and low.

A bigger place in the sun was to be achieved so that the German nation could continue to grow and unfold.  This sense of growth and destiny pervaded Berlin in the 1890's and the city was caught up in a swirl of international plans and action.  Groener was exhilarated by such grand tempo although he also observed that much of the political and intellectual activity originated from the ranks of the dissatisfied.  The German scene toward the end of the nineteenth century reflected both zealous commercial optimism and bilious political discontent, and the booming Empire was not exactly building on settled foundations.

The German system still lacked important internal

improvements, both of a mechanical and spiritual nature. The three-class voting system in Prussia insulted modern sensitivities and, in Alsace-Lorraine and Poland, subjects without full German rights wondered when they might be fully dignified by their government. The Empire still lacked an adequate revenue program and property tax rights remained within the shelter of regional state authority. The junkers were not willing to submit their estates to national regulation, and in Prussia they easily controlled state laws and maintained their property tax immunities. The military budget periodically raised questions of ultimate constitutional authority in the Reichstag and always the Kaiser prevailed as the absolute war lord. He could remind the Reichstag that its part in the military budget was a privilege conceded by the crown and not a right with final powers. Since the bourgeois parties feared socialism even more than they resented junker leadership, it remained possible for the conservative force to keep Reichstag alignments fluid and maintain their form of constitutional authority. Socialism was of course anathema, but any bourgeois Reichstag influence was also to be checked for it represented national integration and the end of particularist privileges and autonomies.

Under William II the junkers remained in formidable position as the Bundesrat, bureaucracy, and army remained under aristocratic control. The Bundesrat could initiate and veto Empire legislation, and the army could impose martial law at the Kaiser's command. Legally and militarily, Germany was well hobbled by the Bismarkian constitution.[6] But the Reichstag and the socialists continued to increase their pressure and many junkers sensed that the conservative dike could not forever hold back the tide of the modern, alien society. Estates were falling into bourgeois hands and the city politicians were coming into the Prussian villages. Many of the young aristocrats even began to feel and talk in terms of new equalities although not yet ready to forfeit the traditional privileges. Groener first came in contact with this junker class in the early 1890's and he suggested novelist Theodore Fontane as a most intimate authority on the mood and problems of the Prussian junker in the final decades of the nineteenth century.

Fontane was both a friend and a critic of the nineteenth

century Prussian junker and his analysis has some claim to
fair-minded intelligence. A brief synopsis might be assayed
as follows:  Once the junker class was secure on the land
and of vital service to the state it fought resolutely for the
King and governed the countryside with no little integrity and
progressiveness.  The exaggerated disciplinary style was
even culturally helpful in a primitive setting, but in the nineteenth century the effects of economic and political change
began to eat into their rural patrimony.  Bourgeois money.
ideas, even girl friends drifted into the junker life and the
younger generation began to lose its self-assurance.  No
longer vital to society, their class sensitivity was often
overdrawn and their noble or authoritarian mannerisms bor-
dered on the caricature.  They were going out of style and
they sensed it.  A frivolous life with the Guards or an occasional duel did not successfully replace respectable purpose or ethical honor.

In a memorable scene Fontane portrayed the growing
political estrangement of the junker from the modern scene.
Dubslav Stechlin, an ideal type with a sincere feeling for
his fellow man, allowed himself to be entered in a Reichstag
electoral contest but his inept conservative backers could not
muster majority support.  The villagers voted for a Social
Democrat from Berlin who neither knew them nor, thought
Stechlin, understood their problems. The election was a social story in itself as the stiff old nobles sat around awk-
wardly in their inn and awaited results. Even wise old Stechlin cast his vote with the snorting comment, "I'll just have
to go along with this foolishness." The new political world
of speeches and popularity was entirely strange to the junker
nature. After their man lost, Stechlin's backers retired to a
fine dinner, toasted the King and Kaiser, and scattered to
their manor homes in their coaches. The world might be moving toward foolish democracy but on their estates they could
still maintain the old way of life and hope that the deluge
might yet be delayed awhile.

This Fontane picture described the mood and setting of
the Prussian governing class, increasingly out of step with
social change in modern Germany, but also instinctively
stubborn and obtuse about self-liquidating reform.  The
Groener's were accepted in the Imperial Army as long as they

served the Prussian Hohenzollern. Any broader concept of German patriotism must be subordinate, not superior, to that dynasty which still represented junker control. Groener's rejection of the Kaiser's authority in November, 1918, symbolized the formal end of such junker sovereignty and identified him with the end of an age. This was the ideological import of his role at Spa in 1918 and the reason for conservative bitterness against him. Defeat and abdication meant the end of their rule and it was irrelevant to them that his heart was also monarchic and strongly attached to the Prussian General Staff. They resented him all the more as an alien spirit within the very Hohenzollern council. His national patriotism rising above any particular dynasty was directed by bourgeois realism and Swabian flexibility. Such values were meaningless to the junker credo and to Hohenzollern egocentricity. As Chancellor Hohenlohe once remarked in the 1890's, these Prussian nobles "cared nothing about the Reich and would rather sacrifice it today than tomorrow." And a pure Prussian like Schlieffen could also idly observe that the Swabians were "honestly German-minded, in any case more honestly than we Prussians."[7]

Prussian absolutism was an anomalous, yet dominating relic among the Empire materialists, scientists, and seekers of truth. "Durch Gottes Gnade bin ich was ich bin," began the service which was read to young William II as he prepared to open his first Reichstag. On such an occasion one may suspect that his sense of Grace entailed more power than humility. The many hard-minded Germans did not believe in such mysticism but they were happy to accept the power and prosperity which the Hohenzollern Empire generated. But the Kaiser and his Prussian lords apparently did believe in the special righteousness of their authority, either as divine destiny or as historical merit. A proud and fierce man like Bismarck was committed to a concept of personal fealty. "I will stand or fall with my own liege lord," he could say, "even if, in my opinion, he foolishly commits me to destruction." Or as junker Oldenbourg-Januschau told Wuerttemberger Conrad Haussmann in the Daily Telegraph debate in 1908: "... we are different in yet another conception: for you the Kaiser is an institution. For us he is a person. And we will serve His Majesty the Kaiser personally as long as

we live, without fear, but until the last breath, in the old
loyalty which we have never denied him." It was the same
Januschau who once remarked that the King of Prussia must
at all times be in a position to tell a lieutenant, "Take ten
men and close the Reichstag." In their growing sense of
estrangement and even isolation, quite a few of the Januschau
group hoped that such a miraculous deed might yet come to
pass. [8]

The Groeners did not swear to single men, but their
young lieutenant at the War Academy was not bothered by
such constitutional questions. He was a happy soldier in a
vibrant, exciting world capital. He merged into his new
Prussian environment and regarded certain Swabian distinctions as mere localisms which had no bearing on his career
or on his patriotism. The question of the Empire's survival,
or the Kaiser's authority, certainly never crossed his mind.
Once he went through the red tape of applying for an invitation to a royal ball. Lieutenants were in the sixty-second,
and last, rank of those who were eligible for such a select
affair. University rectors, incidentally, were in the forty-
seventh rank. Everyone had to be in uniform and for those
luckless enough to be without one, the Kaiser had designed
a special costume. It consisted of lacquered shoes with
buckle, long white stockings which merged into knee pants
under a colorful frock. No wonder old Chancellor Hohenlohe
was so concerned about somehow qualifying for the right to
wear a uniform.

Groener was probably somewhat awed by the glitter and
show of such an Imperial gathering. The Kaiser's palace on
the Spree had been lavishly refinished, in glaring contrast
to the relative simplicity of previous Hohenzollern residences.
William had to do everything different and bigger. But the
sumptuous and impersonal theatrics of the royal ball left
Groener rather hollow and bored. Wuerttemberg's royal re-
ceptions had been so much smaller and graciously intimate.
There it was apparently not uncommon for a young lieutenant
to argue out his seating rank with the court steward, and at
the close, many groups would leave and continue the party
at a nearby hotel or inn. But the Imperial palace was not
Ludwigsburg and Groener wandered around rather lost. He
watched the red-jacketed Guards swirl their highly trained

dancing skill and he picked up a hat for a dignified old government official who was too tightly corseted to make the
effort himself.

A Prussian junker, wandering through the same royal
palace, could tell of his deep reverence before the mementos
and grandeur of the Prussian past as it was represented in
those halls. The boy who gamboled in the streets of Ulm and
later parried wits with the burghers of Schwaebisch-Gmuend
could hardly be thus affected. He would become a disciple
of Schlieffen and a devoted member of the General Staff, and
his loyalty to them would prevail. This was the tradition
which would absorb the best years, and dreams, of his life.
He regarded the Empire and the army as integrated German
institutions, regardless of past origins or contesting particularistic sentiment, but he would regard the General Staff as
a national resource, not a hereditary Prussian possession.
Such expanded unity excited his nationalist spirit and served
his professional ambition.

The Prussian soldier cannot simply be identified with
the general maladjustment of his class. Old Moltke and
Schlieffen lived long and active lives, and the Imperial army
of the twentieth century was still their handiwork. Its quality
would be successfully demonstrated in World War I. The
Kaiser had meddled here, as elsewhere, but the organization
had its own deep tradition, and a world situation forced its
work and galvanized its spirit. This army and its junker
leaders had a critical, ever-changing job to do and thus they
maintained both their progressive energy and their status in
society. As German diplomacy stumbled after 1890, more
and more Germans began to regard their General Staff and
army as the emergency trump. After the Moroccan crisis and
evident German interest in stronger armament as evinced by
the elections of 1907, even the socialists began to speak of
modernizing and improving, rather than dismantling, the Empire army. This key position of Prussian strength, under absolute royal command, was thus left increasingly free of
criticism and its entrenched importance in public affairs
greatly buttressed conservative interests in the national political arena.

Several Empire elections were decided in favor of the
administration when some crisis persuaded patriotic unity or

when it seemed that the Reichstag critics were slighting armament needs. A thorough tax reform bill was consistently postponed on the grounds that it would dangerously anger the junker element in and out of the army, and a constitution for Alsace-Lorraine was postponed in 1913 because the army took advantage of the Schnabele affair to continue its martial authority along the French frontier.[9]  The Kaiser and his army represented the final great bastions of junker strength in an industrializing society pressing for modern constitutional change.

These facets of the Prussian world illustrate the new environment into which young Lieutenant Groener was moving. Bred to different values, he would nonetheless respect and adopt much of the Prussian training. Without resenting junker priorities, he trusted quietly in his own talents and prepared to push through whatever path he might be enabled to follow. His very rank and presence at the Academy indicated that democratic advance was possible in the Imperial army and he quickly developed an unbegrudging admiration for the Prussian military tradition. And no one would question his disparate origins until he began to reflect upon them in that future time of crisis and decision.

Groener entered the War Academy in 1893 on the very eve of basic diplomatic and strategic changes for Germany. The Franco-Russian alliance was nearing reality and the diplomatic fortunes of the Empire were about to go into reverse. The subsequent two-front dilemma would then compel a radical change in Germany's military strategy. Schlieffen's flanking idea was in evidence as early as 1891 but it would not fully go on the General Staff planning board until 1894-1895. Groener's higher strategic education would take place during those years of new planning and, by design or not, some of his Academy work was not unrelated to General Staff problems and studies of the day.

The Academy, for all of its elevated implications, enjoyed neither Imperial favor nor army respect. It had the job of giving advanced theoretical training to selected military personnel and yet such work was not taken too seriously. The Kaiser wanted to deflate the vaunted General Staff and once again elevate the corps commanders to primary status, illustrating his penchant for giving the important positions to those less astute and brainy. He was more interested in having the key officials personally amenable to himself. The field commanders were naturally encouraged by such a royal attitude and they also tended to sneer at Academy theory. The Kaiser was chary with fiscal support and the regular units sent instructors to the Academy who had neither the ability nor the inclination to teach. Schlieffen was aware of such impediments and he simply picked out the best of the Academy students and finished their training in the Staff itself. The Academy classrooms apparently reflected such multiple disinterest and Groener remembered that he often read newspapers or wrote letters during class sessions. But Prussian experience and application showed through despite such indifference and he received effective instruction in such subjects as military history, terrain study, supply problems, and procedures in tactics and strategy.

In a three-year sequence, the students worked through the command assignments of a brigade, division, and corps. Military history moved primarily from classical campaigns to the strategy of Frederick the Great, Napoleon, and Moltke. The final year was devoted especially to the strategy of Moltke, as it was recent enough for detailed work and contemporary relevance. Groener and his classmates were taught to appreciate the merits of a tough defense and yet the stress was placed on offense. Frederick, Napoleon, and Moltke were the venerated masters and all of them exemplified intelligent daring and the sacred fire of command. The campaigns of Moltke especially demonstrated the speedy military resolution of complicated political problems. Destruction was minimal and his wars were regarded as artistic duels in which struggle and civility were happily related. The German military leaders thereafter tended to look on war as an instinctive, scientific, and artistic exercise. The best plan and the most skillful execution prevailed; problems were solved and life rejuvenated.

Europe's competitive principle of life was yet in high noon and the happily successful Germans were in proud accord with such a world. Moltke was a thoroughly cultivated and humane person who thought the dream of eternal peace to be both foolish and ugly. Struggle was an integral part of human nature and international wars could most mercifully be

controlled by rapid, conclusive engagement. He could en-
vision the massive sacrifice of the next war although the
magnitude and reality of such mass slaughter were of course
not fully impressed on these contemporaries of Bismarck.
He was the diplomat who knew how to end wars and thus give
them strategic sense. Moltke's intellectual heirs would find
that they could neither win their war nor end it.

One especially interesting item in Groener's Academy
experience involved Frederick the Great and the Seven Years
War. The class considered the Prussian King's act of war
against Maria Theresa in 1756. Frederick was informed that
his enemies would attack him in the Spring of 1757. He decided to strike first, going through neutral Saxony in order
to break most quickly into Bohemia. But he attacked only
after first delivering a fourteen-day ultimatum to Austria.
The military writer, Bernhardi, maintained that Frederick
should have moved immediately without a prior ultimatum.
The class was asked to discuss this Bernhardi criticism in
a written examination.

Groener's answer disagreed with Bernhardi. He pointed
out that those fourteen days did not worsen the military situation. They did not diminish the chance for victory and Frederick's position was so unfavorable that he could well afford
to wait a few more days for some possible diplomatic assistance. And the waiting period gave the Prussians a chance
for full military preparation behind a veil of diplomatic negotiation. [10] His answer reflected clever patience and opportunism, qualities which were of course easier to phrase
than to practice. For in the July crisis of 1914, Groener
would also say to the mobilization question, "better today,
than tomorrow."

The Academy strategist had no argument with Frederick's
march through Saxony and he did not try to justify it with any
legalistic or moralistic logic. Such a radical move seemed
critically necessary to victory and thus to be ventured. He
sifted the various choices open to the Prussian King and then
made his choice. The rights of the enemy were not denied,
they were simply opposed. Such a frankness and integrity
of mind would characterize Groener throughout his life. Recognizing that there were other alternatives and other rights
in the world of war and politics, he claimed only the right

to decide and assert his own interest. Tactics, strength, and fate might then decide the victory and arbitrate between the domestic political parties.

In his final Academy year Groener worked on a projected encirclement and investment of Epinal. In that problem he began to comprehend the formidable requirements of a break-through operation against a modern fortification line. The siege of Sevastapol in the Crimean War furnished the historical lesson to that particular Groener study, and a few years later the Russo-Japanese stalemate at Mukden confirmed his conclusions. Mounting and relentless pressure, in men and materiel, seemed necessary in a tedious, exhausting operation. Groener favored wider flanking tactics to loosen up the defense and he argued his point with those Academy classmates who supported the power penetration. Such discussion by the neophytes echoed the actual problem facing the General Staff at that very time. Schlieffen was already at work on his flanking plan since it seemed increasingly clear that a penetration of the French line would cost too much time and manpower. He was not afraid to lose men but the question of time now seemed even more important.

The two-front dilemma was a reality and quick offensive victory in the west appeared to be the logical first assignment for the German army. Groener already favored the broad, advancing front in the Academy classrooms and he would convert easily to the celebrated flanking scheme of Schlieffen. That plan, and the figure of Schlieffen, would captivate the military admiration of Groener for the rest of his life. Its radical logic characterized his militant spirit until 1917 and then it represented an unvarying exception to subsequent caution and political sophistication.

Groener's Academy work in such key subjects as tactics, military history and General Staff duty was superior, and he was rewarded with an assignment to the topographic section of General Staff headquarters. It was recognized as a promising entry into that inner sanctum where Schlieffen and his aides functioned as the brain cell of the German army. There he could train his eye for the landscape and develop the intimacy with map work so increasingly vital to the management of massive and far-flung armies. Groener's first summer of map work took him into the Lueneberger Heath where he assembled his data and communed with nature. But the ambitious little Swabian also saved on his expense money and made week-end trips to Bremen and Hamburg. There he studied and sketched dock facilities.

Germany's world policy was under way and the possibility of a future shipping problem was not overlooked. And his visits were not wasted for he later directed the railroad assembly of the German Boxer expeditionary force, which embarked in Hamburg. On his second summer assignment he was sent far away from any major cities, so he spent his spare time in the nearby taverns and hobnobbed with the natives. Such grassroot habits were natural to him and he stayed on friendly footing with the common man even though his military career and Prussian influences led him definitely toward authoritarian principles of leadership. Groener would believe in democratic feeling and behavior much more than he would ever believe in democratic authority.

During the winters of those first post-Academy years, Groener prepared his maps and worked on self-assigned tactical projects. He was merely on attached service with General Staff headquarters and hopefully alert for the chance to show his quality and receive a regular appointment to this highest command post. He and others in the topographic section helped out with various aspects of Staff duties along with their own specific mapping chores. Periodically they were handed special strategic problems and were evaluated on their performance. Here lay the big chance to make an impression. Groener's first winter exercise raised no eyebrows, and the following winter his answer to a strategic problem was rated last by the major who supervised the examination. But a general, First Quartermaster von Alten, a trusted intimate of Schlieffen, reviewed the papers and moved Groener up to first. Dame Fortune had suddenly smiled on Groener and the Chief himself was made aware of his talent.

Groener had not allowed Marshal Bazaine to retreat across the Mosel toward Paris without first scoring a rearguard victory and perhaps this bit of aggressive defense marked him as a man of proper fire and foresight. He was appointed to General Staff headquarters on March 25, 1899, and assigned duty in the railroad section. That very year witnessed the first official decision to route the German advance through Belgium and Groener's railroad work became immediately involved in the Schlieffen Plan. Its life was Henceforth intertwined with his own.

Thus Groener moved into another stage of his life. The Berlin sally had been wondrously rewarding and now he functioned on high Empire levels. A man of Swabian breeding and Prussian training, he represented the sort of integration with which the German Empire might be happy. As a soldier he was both monarchic and democratic in social outlook. He knew major parts of the Empire and comprehended the German conglomeration; but he also assumed a continuing unification process and he subscribed almost unconsciously to a national patriotism which was above regional or class sentiment. [11]

# CHAPTER TWO

## In The General Staff

The Prussian army helped to liberate Germany from Napoleon and it facilitated the national unification under Bismarck. Its military service and logic seemed well suited to the national interest. The Napoleonic experience created the need and will for national self-assertion in a world of obvious insecurity. Hegel would now declare that self-defense was the first requirement of any state and Clausewitz could agree that "all else can be regarded, strictly speaking, as _faux frais_. German thought would begin to idealize the nature of the state even as it had earlier idealized the sovereignty of the spirit. Hegel's first great work dealt with the phenomenology of the spirit. By mid-century, Ranke was giving discourse on the phenomenology of the state. And by 1900, Treitschke and others understood national life almost as a biological organism with its right to fight for life and growth. Such competitive naturalism was certainly not unique to German thought but it was here perhaps more ebulliently glorified than among other more settled and experienced nations. [1]

The far-flung campaigns of the Napoleonic wars impressed on all the contestants a need for informed and ramified military planning. In Prussia such a study section was first set up in the reorganization of the War Ministry in 1814. For the next forty-five years this General Staff office occupied a position of academic modesty and administrative subordinancy within the framework of the War Ministry. Its geodetic surveys and studies in war history impressed few people and the regular army regarded it primarily as a research service. The army commanders were much more interested in once again working clear of War Ministry supervision and re-establishing their direct relationship with the King. The Prussian conservatives resisted the reform concepts of Boyen and Gneisenau and they successfully blocked the authority of the War Ministry and the development of a militia army. The fighting quality of the civilian reserves was found to be inferior in the Revolution of 1848-1849 and the resultant reorganization of the Prussian army under Roon again entrenched the King and his generals beyond the reach of the government and the people.

The spectacular role of the Prussian military in the German unification seemed to justify their place in the state and most German patriots were thereafter willing to overlook residual junker privileges and the army's immunity from civilian supervision. As William II could say to the Chancellor of the Empire in the 1890's, "The army and its internal features do not concern the State Ministry at all, since the constitution specifically reserves these for the King's sole jurisdiction."[2]     This immunity of ruler and army from the jurisdiction of the national government represented the basic autocracy and militarism of the second German Empire. The Hohenzollern authority was constitutionally entrenched by his control of the Empire's Upper House (Bundesrat) and by his direct command over the German army. Legal reform was a practical impossibility as long as the Prussian King and the Prussian aristocrats were thus in control of the Empire machinery.

The man who best justified such modern military privilege also first brought the General Staff to a position of public prominence. Moltke was still head of an academic General Staff as the Danish War broke out in 1864. In fact, he was almost left home in Berlin. Then his corrective views on painful German blunders in the field impressed the King and his status was decisively enhanced. On the very eve of the war with Austria in 1866, he was placed in command of all the Prussian armies. His victory at Koeniggraetz, and later at Sedan in 1870, fully established the General Staff as a scholarly and scientific master of war. Scientific preparation and nervy calculation were seemingly blended into an invincible instrument of German force. Under the leadership of Moltke and Bismarck, the risk and pain of war seemed advantageous and permissible to national policy. German interests were advanced and yet also regulated. The German army was praised as the first institution of the Empire, but it was also kept subordinate to the political will of Bismarck. In many German eyes it did seem that the Darwinistic necessities of life were under successful and civilized management. A highly cultivated and humane man, such as Moltke, could say with stoical equanimity, "Eternal peace is a dream and not even a fine one, and war is a link in God's world order." Without war, man would become bogged down in idle materialism.[3]

For Bismarck and Moltke such a readiness to fight expressed the controlled instinct of sophisticated leaders. Their experience with war had not been catastrophic. Their will helped to excite a comparable public militancy but their shrewdness and wisdom could not be as easily popularized. Mass ego, mass interest, and mass means could exaggerate their competitive daring into uncontrollable violence, especially when sparked by a jingoistic ruler and directed by soldierly logic.

The Imperial Army's assignment after the wars of unification continued to be formidable and yet it was not desperate. The French were weak and the eastern Empires were diplomatically attached to Germany. The feared two-front war remained a realistic possibility and yet Moltke's margin of security seemed adequate. The Russian army was judged awkward enough to be kept at bay and the German defensive position between Switzerland and Luxembourg seemed much too difficult for any French break-through. Even should such a two-front war develop, it was confidently expected that the German army could hold its position with mobile defensive tactics and wait for a diplomatic solution. The quick offensive elimination of France seemed highly improbable to Moltke and he was not inclined to lose his force in Russian space.[4] He would rely on powerful defensive sallies and Bismarck's diplomacy. Such an aggressive defense seemed cogent as long as Russian ineptitude and Bismarckian mastery continued, but after 1890 conditions changed.

Bismarck was removed and, with French help, Russian striking power was modernized. The French-Russian alliance in 1894 made grim reality out of what had been a mere hypothetical two-front problem. Germany's hegemony power was suddenly brought back into European balance and its new leaders were confronted by resentful and suspicious neighbors. German diplomacy could not maneuver its way clear of such hostile currents and the German army was forced to face up to a grave new assignment. And in its predicament, this army adopted a more radical strategy and committed its nation to a role of irrational desperation in the wars to come.

The Chief of Staff who had to solve the problem of encirclement was Schlieffen. Like Moltke, he featured a quiet manner and tireless industry. Sphynx-like even among his colleagues, he demonstrated a discreet public behavior and and a co-operative propriety in his Staff's relationship with the other agencies of government. In this respect he differed radically from his immediate predecessor, Waldersee, who flitted constantly about the political wings to demonstrate the sort of mischief which was possible in a government which tolerated private military channels of command responsibility. Schlieffen's part in the encouragement of militaristic influence lay in his fascinating strategic thought, not in any opportunistic use of his office or person. This man of simple piety and patient professional progress would study the problem of a two-front war and commit his army to a radical, aggressive gamble. He would sweep through neutral Belgium and defeat France in six to eight weeks. Then he would shift his strength to the east and frustrate the Russian enemy.

Schlieffen's first memorandum as Chief of Staff, in 1891, reflected a will for aggressive, conclusive action. He ruefully granted that the French defensive line was difficult and that a "decision" might have to be sought in the east. It was too bad that the German and Austrian forces could not be immediately consolidated, for then they could knock out the French. Of course, another tactic might simply be to outflank the French line by way of Belgium. Schlieffen's mind already entertained notions of immediate, or complete, victory on a particular front. Moltke was willing to defend and wait for a diplomatic solution. But he had Bismarck, and his two-front problems remained theoretical. Schlieffen's predicament was actual and his response was less cautious.

He knew that the French and Russian armies were improving and he also realized that industrial Germany would find it difficult to sustain a long war.  He placed little reliance in his Austrian ally and the German navy admitted its inability to be of any effective assistance in a western campaign. Schlieffen had a prime army and he decided to commit it absolutely.  Maybe such Prussian directness reflected the strength and limitations of his forefathers and he was less subtle and complex than Moltke.  Maybe his memory of the Prussian hymn of victory on the heights of Koeniggratz fostered his dream of another complete triumph.  Certainly his military responsibility was difficult and, just as certainly, his strategic solution would prove to be of far-reaching consequence to subsequent German history.[5]

Schlieffen worked on his western offensive for the rest of that decade.  He studied a vital penetration at Nancy since such a drive would also force a decisive French stand, but it threatened to take too much time and expose the German east to the expected Russian invasion.  A lead-off action against Russia could hardly end in a quick victory and Schlieffen placed little stock in any meaningful Austrian cooperation.  He trusted nothing except his own army and his own developing plan.  In 1897 he projected, and abandoned, a button-hook operation around Verdun since broad rail support could not be mustered there and the proximity of the Belgian border hindered a broad thrust.  Any forceful French counter-attack toward Belgium would break the slender German prong.  Then he decided that, "Any offensive which wants to turn around Verdun must not be afraid to violate the neutrality of Luxembourg, nor even that of Belgium."  He decided that neutral sanctities could not be allowed to restrict the German chance and in 1899 he projected his army's drive into France by way of Belgium.

Once the moral violation was digested, the advantage of an even deeper flank through Lille would not long be disregarded.  The superior rail net west of the Meuse could then be used to give effective supply support to the entire flank, especially along its outside line.  Thus the expansive German rail facilities along the lower Rhine could be switched through Liege and Brussels toward the open French frontier, with excellent road and rail systems continuing all the way to Paris.  The speedy, mass movement so vital to Schlieffen's flanking force might here find its decisive logistical support. Thus not only the tough French fortification line,  but also the superior German-Belgian rail net, drew Schlieffen's offensive plans ever more to the northwest.  "In other words," he said to his Staff in 1904,  "one attacks along the front Verdun-Lille, not Belfort-Verdun, for that much expansion will be generally necessary in order to get enough room for free mobility." The General Staff had arrived at its solution to Germany's two-front predicament.

The addition of Britain as another possible enemy did not change the plans for a march on Paris.  It was not expected to be able to block a German land operation and the Schlieffen Staff simply felt itself forced to shrug off the maritime implications of any British opposition.  It saw no other recourse against the probable coalition.  Defensive action seemed even more hopeless and the German army chose to force its opportunity rather than wait for two-front pressure. Such grim, combative logic ruled out certain moral intangibles which might accrue to a German defense and it discounted the chance of any diplomatic relief.  The Schlieffen Plan chose to assert German strength rather than await a pleasant diplomatic surprise. [6]

The reaction of the Imperial government was a classic in self-revelation.  Schlieffen was no frondeur and he passed his Belgian project into the private channels which conveyed so much of the Empire's business.  Schlieffen was a good friend of Holstein but,  according to recorded memory,  he chose to give him cognizance of the plan by way of that veteran liaison expert, Hutten-Czapski, who was close to both Holstein and Chancellor Hohenlohe,  and was expected to get their reaction to the Belgian plan.  It was in 1899 that Czapski took Schlieffen's plan to Holstein and asked for the latter's judgment on the neutrality violation.  The question was crucial and almost worth a council of state.  But Holstein took the burden on himself,  thought seriously for awhile and told Czapski,  "If the Chief of Staff, especially a strategic authority such as Schlieffen,  believes such a measure to be necessary, then it is the obligation of diplomacy to adjust to it and prepare for it in every possible way." Holstein spoke with his aged advisee, Hohenlohe,  on the following morning and a few days later Schlieffen was invited to dine with the Chancellor in the company of other friends. There the Chief of Staff and Hohenlohe retired for a private conversation. Schlieffen was thereafter at ease with his project and undoubtedly it was given verbal sanction. It would not be seriously weighted again by government officils until 1913.[7]

One wonders whether Schlieffen and Holstein had not privately discussed their problem before the Czapski action. Holstein's relatively quick response to such a question and his fatuous praise of Schlieffen seem worthy of some suspicion. He and Schlieffen met almost weekly in long dinner sessions during those years and one wonders why the general had to convey his plan by way of Czapski. Such curiosity notwithstanding, the rather informal and secretive acceptance by the government of such an explosive piece of strategy speaks volumes about its devious personal methods and its fantastic submission to radical military logic.

Schlieffen's strategy placed a campaign victory above deeper diplomatic and technological considerations. The fall of Paris could not defeat Britain and the latter's naval blockade would then presumably strangle Germany's economic capacity for a longer struggle. Admiral Tirpitz admitted his helplessness on the blockade problem and German government officials did not expect their nation to be able to sustain more than an eighteen-month war effort. Yet the German diplomatic position, especially after the French-British Entente, was so perplexing that a desperate strike for relief and realignment was for a time seriously considered. In 1904 the unilateral French advance in Morocco angered German pride and Berlin pressed for some compensation, preferably a port along the North African coast. Russia was busy with its Japanese war and France seemed to be momentarily isolated, but Britain's maritime sensitivities were aroused and she stepped resolutely to the side of her new colonial ally, France. Holstein wanted to push German demands to the brink but Chancellor Buelow accepted international arbitration after two letters from the Kaiser warned him that the army and navy were not ready, and the socialists were still a dangerous problem.

On New Year's Day, 1906, the mercurial ruler had to tell his disappointed generals that there would be no war.

They were ready to undertake a military recovery of the German decline and Schlieffen admitted, in 1904, that the Moroccan crisis presented an opportune moment, "should the necessity for a war with France reveal itself." But apparently neither he nor his Kaiser directly pressed for war in the climax months of 1905-1906. Nevertheless, that crisis did present a situation and an atmosphere of tension, which gave special, suggestive meaning to Schlieffen's full and classic formulation of his plan.[8]

In the Fall of 1905, Schlieffen lectured to his Staff on Napoleon's campaign against Prussia in 1806. Most of the French power was concentrated on the right flank between Bamberg and Bayreuth. With the opening of hostilities, Napoleon directed this flank toward Berlin. The same move separated that capital from its western armies and drove a wedge between the Prussian force and its potential ally, Russia. An attack straight into the western gateway to Prussia would have allowed its army to recoil back onto its own base and probably Russian support. The strike for a capital city was a favorite tactic of Napoleon, forcing the enemy to make a stand and producing a quick victory decision.

Napoleon's right flank was directly up against Hapsburg Bohemia and a neutrality violation by his advancing troops seemed possible. Critics might censure the French emperor for so flagrantly risking Austrian intervention, but Schlieffen discounted such criticism. The right flank was Napoleon's vital force and he employed it despite risk, because he was confident that it would bring victory. Its positive action and prospect was not to be governed by Austrian decision. Napoleon stayed with his own plan for quick victory; he had the will to act with positive force, not negative considerations. Schlieffen urged his Staff to learn from the Napoleonic example. Germany must emulate its method and multiply its force. Like Napoleon, the German commanders must have the strength and nerve to force their plan on the enemy.

In January, 1906, the barely retired Schlieffen finished his celebrated memorandum on an operation into Belgium and France. The Moroccan negotiations during those winter months did give a certain crisis impetus to his work and already he feared that his successor, the younger Moltke, would not stress the flanking force enough.

Schlieffen's memorandum described France as a great fortress. It had an almost impenetrable defensive line from Belfort to Mezieres. A second defensive arc behind Mezieres extended from Verdun through Rheims to La Fere. Such fortification lines were formidable obstacles and would undoubtedly tie up any German frontal assault. And the recent Russo-Japanese war showed how maneuvering armies could lock themselves in paralyzing trench war. Germany must avoid such a stalemate because it had neither the position nor the resources for such a test of strength. The entire French defensive complex was to be outflanked by way of Belgium. The northern wing would jump off through the Liege area and fan out to the south and west over Namur and Brussels. Direction was to be maintained toward Lille and Northwestern France. Thus a flanking grip on the defending line could be maintained and the envelopment continued. The French defense was to be hooked in from behind and rolled up toward the Swiss frontier. Strongholds were to be by-passed and mopped up by follow-up lines of the advance. The "colossal fortress" of Paris was to be encircled from the southwest.

This memorandum did not promise victory; indeed it forecast failure unless certain improvements were made. The Metz fortress position was not deeply buttressed enough to securely anchor the long right flank and also hold planned German defensive traps in Alsace-Lorraine. The army lacked sufficient heavy artillery to smash through fortification points, and eight more corps were needed if that right flank was to have the controlling force it needed to flood Belgium and envelope Paris. It must have the power to push through any defensive stand and peel off those units necessary to the investment of by-passed strongpoints. Man power was the critical problem and it was on this point that Schlieffen was most uncertain. Approach Paris as they might, he wrote,

"we will soon recognize that we are too weak for a continuation of the operation in this direction. We will find the experience of all earlier conquerors certified: that offensive war requires and uses up much strength, that such gets constantly weaker as that of the defender increases and all this especially in a land which bristles with fortifications.

> ... It is therefore necessary that the Germans be
> as strong as possible on the right flank, for here
> the decisive battle may be expected."

Thus did Schlieffen define and bequeath his thought to his erstwhile Staff and it remained the governing idea of subsequent German strategy.

Gerhard Ritter's critique, and publication of the various Schlieffen Plan fragments, has now brought the Schlieffen controversy to a new level of understanding. It is quite evident that Schlieffen recognized the formidable problems which would be involved in the success of such a massive envelopment. Repeatedly he admitted that the German force would find itself too weak. Liege and the Belgian railroads must fall substantially preserved into German hands or the entire operation would be without a sound logistical base. The prospect of reducing Paris seemed slight and the English army was not even mentioned in the main memorandum. A supplementary fragment then followed in which the British force, almost as an afterthought, was to be locked into its Channel ports. Maritime implications of Britain's presence in the war were not brought into the discussion; such problems lay beyond army range and were simply left to the gods. And Schlieffen's bold project assumed no help from either Austria or his own fleet. His army must address and solve its problem as though no other help was possible. In such assumption he was not entirely unrealistic but his will to triumph a la Napoleon, instead of a la Frederick, would prove to be a fatal German gamble. Not only was his army prepared to fight alone but it was permitted to shape its plan without the serious consultation of German naval, or economic, or political leaders. Here was a classic example of militaristic logic in control of national policy.[9]

William Groener would say, even after 1918, that the Schlieffen Plan's only fault lay in its mismanaged failure in 1914; it was strategically sound and morally comprehensible. But Gerhard Ritter has declared this plan to be not only mechanically unrealistic but also psychologically fatal to subsequent German history. It committed Germany to an immoral blunder and gave seeming justice to the Allied cause and the Allied peace. It began that isolation of the German position, moral and physical, which led to further desperation and even deeper alienation from the spirit and body of western Europe. For Ritter, the Schlieffen Plan was a foolish and fatal action, pregnant with military imprudence and moral disregard.

William Groener's years in the General Staff paralleled the Imperial life and failure of the Schlieffen Plan. He participated in its construction from 1899 until 1914 and he subscribed to its thought with trust and admiration. He was receptive to war in 1905 and he agreed with Schlieffen that Germany's diplomatic perplexities could only be relieved by bold action. Certain problems could not be unravelled; they had to be cut through and he was willing to assay the strike.

Groener was assigned to the railroad section of the General Staff and it was here that he became intimately involved with the Schlieffen Plan. Such railroad work meant much timetable drudgery and it was one of those technical chores generally avoided by those who had the pedigree for Guard or cavalry units. The new bourgeois officers in the Imperial army were frequently posted at such less exciting positions and thus unwittingly trained for leadership in the technical war to come.

The railroad gave nineteenth century Germany new pivotal force in the life of Europe. It helped to facilitate Prussian economic leadership and it gave the Germans more cohesive military potential. In the clairvoyant words of economist Friedrich List,

> "Speed of mobilization, the rapidity with which troops could be moved from a country's center to its periphery and the other obvious advantages of 'interior lines' of rail transport would be of greater relative advantage to Germany than to any other European country."

Prussian leaders understood this and they began to build such new steel roads. Railroad costs helped to bring about the constitutional crisis which led to Bismarck, and Moltke then used the iron horse to climax German unification on the battlefields of Bohemia and France. He saw that modern mass armies could best be moved and supplied by rail, and his advice was to "build railroads rather than fortresses." His new

German army obtained supervisory authority over all German
rail construction and this influence solidified when most of
the state networks were placed under national control in 1887.
The federal states were usually quite happy to let the army
chart, and finance, railroad development. German rail expansion was thus planned with a studied regard for military
need.

Until 1890 railroad construction centered on Alsace-
Lorraine and southwest Germany, as did Moltke's strategic
interests. Industrial growth and changing military problems
then led to intensified rail expansion in East Prussia, Silesia,
and the Rhineland. The latter area was especially important
to the Schlieffen strategy and, after 1890, six more bridges
and a trans-Eifel network were constructed so that four armies
might be quickly aligned between Trier and Aachen. The
Schlieffen Plan required instantaneous speed, concentrated
volume, and open country for the rapid deployment of a million-man army. Groener and his railroad colleagues would
labor unceasingly to perfect the transportation instrument so
vital to the entire project. Every winter they would pore over
schedules to exact minimum load and speed out of their system. Every year they remodeled the plan as the Staff adjusted
to changing means and problems.

It was tedious and intensive labor with few mistakes
permissible and no opportunity for a meaningful rehearsal.
An antiquated twenty-mile practice track and the yearly corps
maneuver gave the railroad section slight practical experience.
Theirs was a theoretical and bureaucratic preparation, to be
tested by the actual war emergency itself. They were unsung
heroes and not always happy in their role. Such painstaking
drudgery wore on human nature and Groener remarked in his
memoirs, "what person could not understand that the call to
action would be received as a liberation from a long and
wearily borne burden." The desk soldiers wanted to see their
plans in operation too, and, in 1914, Groener would not flick
a muscle of concern as war loomed up. Somehow it seemed
that their repeated labors must also have some purpose and
climax.

Schlieffen's Plan was admittedly beyond the strength of
the German army in 1905, even with Russia momentarily busy
in the Far East. It outlined an operation which might succeed,

if an alerted German government would give its army the
the man power and equipment necessary to such a lightning
blow. Groener very much subscribed to the Schlieffen project and he also understood that it depended on further improvements. He made a supply study of such a flanking
operation in 1906 and his conclusions could hardly be
termed optimistic. He did not share Schlieffen's optimism
about having the advancing armies live off the land. He
reminded the Staff that there would hardly be time to organize supply feeders from the Belgian and French countryside
itself and such magical improvisation could neither be
planned or practiced. The job of maintaining supply contact with a rapidly moving million-man army would be su-
premely difficult and it would demand happy co-ordination
and resourcefulness. The German army had better not plan
on a momentary organization of the Belgian resources but
develop its own supply program instead. There would be
enough need for self-help and improvisation even with successful supply runs from the home front. All would depend
on a systematic rail action which must not be upset by
selfish pressure or special demands from any of the troop
commanders. It was clear that great difficulties would en-
sue "if the railroads are thoroughly destroyed." Harness
teams would not be able to keep up and "the moment would
come when the armies would have to stop and let the supply columns catch up." War had many variables and even
the weatherman could upset the best laid plans. Motor
trucks could effectively bridge the gap between railhead
and front-line, "but it will be a long time before we are in
a position to equip our supply columns with an adequate
number of such transport means."

Groener's memorandum prophetically foresaw that supply contact with a racing front would become increasingly
difficult and that it might only be sustained by means of
motor trucks. They could serve as the connecting rods between the railheads and the forward distribution points.
They were yet experimental in 1906 and, as Groener feared,
they were not yet in adequate supply by 1914. Budgetary
provisions were always stingy and the German High Command was slow to recognize and promote the use of motorized transportation, but its railroad section could not be

accused of obtuseness or technical narrowness on this point. Groener had his finger on the motorized key as early as 1906. [10]

In that same year Groener's railroad section played through a telephone and telegram maneuver in Magdeburg. It was the first large scale exercise for the German soldier in this communication medium. Groener found that shortrange contact between the front combat units was fairly good, but headquarters to the rear had trouble staying in touch with its advance units. Here also, rear echelon contact with a rapidly advancing front was yet an unsolved problem. German telephone and telegram communication was entirely inadequate in 1914. Groener's studies revealed the practical problems of the Schlieffen Plan then and later. He and his Chief recognized that their project was yet unrealistic in 1906; its feasibility in 1914 remained to be tested. But their man power and motorized requirements were never satisfied and the plan would be executed in 1914 without such conditional improvements. Certainly Groener's postwar arguments for the Schlieffen Plan would not be entirely in joint with his own earlier qualifications, and its political shortsightedness seems even greater in the light of such recognized technical deficiencies.

Schlieffen's memorandum of 1906 was finished about a month after his retirement and it represented a summary exposition of his idea. It had now been developed for more than ten years and worked into the German war plan. It magnetized the interest of his subordinates and it would guide Staff planning even after his retirement and death. But the new Chief of Staff, the younger Moltke, also had certain reservations about Schlieffen's concept and he would lean toward more caution. Some of the Schlieffen men in the Staff, including Groener, would be critical of the Moltke alterations and, after the Marne failure, they would hold him responsible for this crucial German set-back. And yet, they all liked Moltke personally and tended to regard him as a noble, misplaced individual.

Groener compared the retirement of Schlieffen to that of Bismarck, as a second major German step downward. Both giants stepped from the stage with reluctance and both were followed by men of lesser training and talent. The professionals were giving way to the favorites in a government controlled by an egotistical dilettante who preferred congenial subordinates to independent professionals. Schlieffen was not without courtly obsequieusness, but he was also an austere, solitary man who could hardly be a companion to the Kaiser. William preferred subordinates who were personally congenial to him, perhaps also intellectually less spry than he. Men like Bismarck and Schlieffen were entirely too sovereign, distant, and entrenched for a Kaiser who loved to banter, scintillate and instruct.

The younger Moltke was an intelligent, sensitive person who tended to oscillate between fear and pride. He was familiar with the elite and relaxed in their company, having served most of his career as an adjutant to his celebrated uncle and to William II. Certainly he did not have the thorough professional experience ordinarily to be desired in a Chief of Staff. His brief troop service was with the preening Guards and his first regimental command was bestowed in 1897. The first review of his unit thrilled him with a sense of exultant authority. He could recite passages from Faust in the midst of some solitary field work and he was excited by the dramatic exploits of Frederick the Great. Occasionally he admitted in his letters that he was a born military leader. Certainly he was flattered with his advancement to the higher echelon and his expressed fear of the job hardly coincided with other statements of interest. He was vice-Chief of Staff for more than two years and expectantly aware of his pending elevation. His appointment was a rather typical act of Imperial favoritism and yet he proved to be a competent Chief, especially with the assistance of the more talented and decisive Ludendorff.

Moltke was not inclined to accept Schlieffen's Plan en toto and it was under his command that Groener undertook his searching supply study. Moltke recognized that the success of such an undertaking would depend on a faultless opening performance and he hardly expected such professional perfection after thirty-five years of peace. Schlieffen apparently expected to surmount all problems with his grand, forcing plan and a self-reliant resourcefulness. Moltke did not believe that will-power could surmount all difficulties and he was much more apprehensive of German chances. "Believe me," he cautioned a more optimistic associate, "too many hounds will kill the hare."

Moltke's strategic thought disagreed with the Schlieffen Plan on two basic points. He was hesitant to risk the entire campaign on a long flanking drive into northwest France. Also he believed in meeting, not circling, the enemy.

The older Moltke had hesitated to wheel into France north of Verdun. He thought such an extended wing would expose the German line of communication to a crippling counter-attack. The younger Moltke also feared a French drive into the German rear. He believed that an exaggerated German commitment in Belgium would leave the middle and upper Rhine dangerously exposed to a French invasion. German industry and the entire back side of the Belgian advance would then come under French guns. The uncle had planned to win in Alsace-Lorraine with a trapping, mobile defensive. The nephew also had his heart set on this theatre and he thought in terms of a balanced pincer strategy out of Belgium and the Vosges. He would commit additional German troop strength to the Vosges front and thus give his line more balanced strength and potential. His Belgian-Lorraine ratio of strength was 3 to 1, whereas the Schlieffen Plan called for a preponderant 7 to 1. However, Moltke's reinforcements on his southern flank were not drawn from the north. They came from the greater man power available to the army after 1905. Thus he did not actually weaken Schlieffen's actual right flank strength. He simply declined to strengthen it further and gave the extra man power to the left flank instead.

The new Chief believed in engaging the enemy. He told his officers that there was little point in marching through Belgium if the French were in Lorraine. The basic purpose of a German move through Belgium was to draw the French out of their fortified eastern front.

> "But if the French come out of their fortress, then they will place themselves in an open field. There is no point... in marching further through Belgium with strong forces when the main French army is advancing in Lorraine. Then only one thought must be considered: to fall on the French army with all possible strength and to strike it wherever it can be found."[11]

Moltke wanted to maneuver with the French and draw them out
for the climatic engagement.  He understood such a tactical
duel as the only normal, sensible way to conduct a campaign.
Schlieffen was not interested in finding the enemy.  He hoped
to move around armies and envelop the entire French defensive
system.  His plan projected a powerful, simple run to the
outside and a consequent enveloping hook.  Moltke's thought
was more cautious and more complicated.  He would open up
with several simultaneous offensives, shuttling troops north
or south as the opportunity presented itself.  He would improvise in the course of the conflict as his uncle had done so
masterfully.  But the younger Moltke lacked the experience
and talent for such intuitive maneuvering and in 1914 he would
soon lose control of his multi-geared offensive.

In Groener's view, the new Chief simply lacked the nerve
to strip Lorraine and gamble with one decisive thrust into
northern France.  He could speak of Schlieffen's feu sacre
but he obviously did not have it.  Once he cried because a
subordinate missed an assignment and the postponement of a
maneuver could make him frantic.  He told his wife on one
such occasion, as rain forced a day's delay, "all the dispo-
sitions can now be thrown aside. ... everything is topsy-turvy
... imagine the consequences if such a forceful intrusion
should occur in a real emergency."[12]  In fact such a last-
minute disturbance did challenge him in 1914 and it brought
him to the verge of collapse.  Neither he nor the Kaiser were
as nervy as they wanted to be and their Faustian dreams were
quite beyond their natures.

Groener worked well under Moltke, even though he regretted the strategic alteration, and he became the head of
the full military railroad section in 1911.  He would push for
final improvements before war broke out in 1914.  Groener
did not spend all of his time with the Staff in Berlin.  There
were tours of line duty in Lorraine and Wuerttemberg.  He also
sailed with the Kaiser's young fleet for a week and then took
a busman's holiday through Holland, Belgium and France.  It
was probably no mere coincidence that he visited those countries which were most related to his Staff work.

In Metz, Groener got a taste of the enemy.  That city
was not reconciled to German control and its resentment pervaded the atmosphere.  The Germans were personae non grata

and the rare cry of "vive le empereur" only served to point up the difference between the city and its ruler.  Those families which could, moved to France when their turn came to provide quarters for the German officers and even Groener's easy good will at the village inn table fell flat.  High and low were alienated by the new authorities.  Abbe Sollin was the spiritual leader of Metz and he moved through the streets with imperious dignity.  And one can imagine that the Kulturkampf did not exactly help to reconcile Alsace-Lorraine to the new German association.  Lorraine was French, of course, and its displeasure had very natural roots, but the German Alsatians were not happy either and their dissatisfaction could not be so easily explained away.  They had native anti-Prussian feelings and some taste for the French culture and yet, the basic impediment to their spiritual reunion with Germany may well have been constitutional.  How could they give their loyalty to a state which denied them equal rights of citizenship?

The German Empire allowed the life of Alsace-Lorraine to be governed by the military interest.  The German soldiers regarded these two provinces as a western glacis, critical to their strategy and thus to be managed in the army's interest. Their desiderata regulated both the native officials and the occupation bureaucrats.  Constitutional protests by the inhabitants were curtly brushed aside and they periodically excited even tighter regulation.  Bismarck understood the two provinces to be military installations and he was not interested in their rights or in their morale.  Let them be unhappy with the Empire. A good bureaucracy was the best constitution they might expect and their pull for more rights was simply reined in.  And when Alsace-Lorraine was finally on the verge of receiving constitutional dignity in 1913, the Zabern affair in Alsace renewed military suspicions and military autocracy in the two provinces.  The Kaiser backed his military authorities to the hilt and constitutional reform was filed away.  Even the resounding Reichstag criticism of the government's action in the Zabern affair merely served to highlight civilian helplessness throughout the Empire.

The Hohenzollern regime shrugged off the popular protest and Chancellor Bethmann-Hollweg blandly told the Reichstag that its vote of censure had no constitutional significance. This was the very man who had sponsored constitutional reform

for Alsace-Lorraine and awaited its fulfillment in 1913. In the
final analysis, this sincere and progressive official remained
a servant to his Kaiser and established dynastic authority.
His first official appearance before the Reichstag in the uniform of a major of the reserve was a highly symbolical act.
It marked his status and his responsibilities in the Prussian
world which bred him. [13]

Groener's company in Metz consisted mostly of young
miners from the Ruhr. Most of them were in sympathy with
socialism and they could hardly be expected to give the Kaiser
the naive loyalty which he requested. They were aware of his
anti-labor tirades and the military leaders were not at all
happy with this increasing volume of recruits from the city.
Some even hesitated to enlarge the army out of fear for this
new social element. Bourgeois officers and proletariat soldiers were still regarded with varying degrees of suspicion by
the junker military leaders.[14]  Would this new breed serve
obediently and accept the traditions of an aristocratic officer
corps? A rising young professional like Groener never entertained such questions about class and tradition and he expected the same uncomplicated patriotism from his men.  He
was happy with his miners, for they served with cheerfulness
and alacrity.

Revolutionary fervor no longer represented the nature of
German socialism.  Increasing prosperity, bargaining rights,
and Reichstag representation were steadily mollifying the opposition mood of the working class.  Unions and shop stewards
were careful to husband their gains and move forward a step
at a time.  Talk of revolution and mass strikes now seemed
foolishly destructive and the mood was distinctly and opti-
mistically for practical progress.  Twentieth century German
socialism was beginning to affiliate its interests with the
larger process of a national society.  It even began to see a
relationship between colonies and competitive economic security and the army was more and more accepted as the shield
of national welfare. Here too a modern German patriotism was
emerging which understood factional objectives to be within
a larger national framework.  Substantial democratic reforms
were still held to be necessary and yet the socialists were
settling into a patient evolutionary gait. [15]

With his Metz company, Groener ran through various

tactical problems under the bright eye of a dynamo named Haeseler. The latter was a Prussian stereotype with a sparse frame, energetic habits, and severe manner. He showed up everywhere, dragging along his crippled foot in a slipper, and only occasionally sitting down to rest in a chair which his servant constantly carried behind him. He liked to experiment with minimal food and sleep for himself, or with night problems and new attack methods for his men. Even the Metz units, stationed at one of Germany's major fortress positions, worked extensively on offensive war. The entire spirit of the Imperial army was one of bold aggressiveness. In fact this was the spirit of the nation. There were problems everywhere, but momentum was yet vibrantly evident and the German will to succeed still set the tone.

Some years later, in 1908, Groener took a week's cruise with the proud but yet insecure "risk" fleet. The General Staff and the Admiralty exchanged such visiting tours of duty in a rather half-hearted attempt to draw the two services together. Many in the General Staff envied the fiscal and publicity talents of Admiral Tirpitz, but they saw no tactical justification for his navy, which took so much money away from the army's budget. Groener enjoyed his sea voyage and he was attracted by sunny skies and a sparkling, running sea. He could sense the lure of the deep. But he soon tired of wake and sky-line, and he turned to assess his friends in blue. They spoke much of Britain and seemed to understand the superity of the foe. Their own force was still in early growth and their experience hardly measured up to the centuries behind the British Jack. Even Tirpitz recognized that his force could not successfully engage with the enemy, and the General Staff came to disregard any possible naval contribution to its strategy. The two service arms did not even communicate their plans to one another, much less correlate them. One bald Moltke comment was rather suggestive of the entire strategic dilemma, "since the navy had no choice for success in a war against Britain, such a war must simply be avoided." Only his own Belgian plan would immediately guarantee such unmanageable opposition. [16]

Germany's prewar mistakes now seem rather obvious and its naval program proved to be especially damaging. It alienated Britain without being able to match such rival sea power. It took much money, and strength, away from the army in the perennial budget negotiations. And it fired up a colony-minded patriotism which helped to pull Germany from its continental sockets into world rivalries for which she lacked basic position.

After his week at sea, Groener continued with a modest tour of the lands to the west. In Rotterdam and Amsterdam he probably scrutinized dock and communication facilities as well as art collections. In Brussels he saw many British visitors and noticed that the Belgians thought nothing of a weekend in Paris. A certain cultural bond between the three nations seemed to exist and it would undoubtedly influence their political policies. Groener was one of those Germans who could not possibly conceive of British neutrality in any German war with France, even if Belgium's neutrality were respected. These western peoples had mutual interests and the British would then simply assist the French at their own strategic convenience, but the Germans would then have forfeited their big offensive chance.

Groener was captivated by Paris and a planned two-week visit stretched into six. The stubby Staff officer in civilian dress sat in the boulevard cafes and watched French life stream by. He liked the French and thought their vivacity to be nicely balanced by a sense for measured form. He watched the visitors from the provinces stand silently and reverently at the tomb of Napoleon. These were the people, and this the tradition, which his German army might some day face in battle. Groener did not notice any militancy or anti-German feeling in the capital. He watched the traditional parade on Bastille Day and the French troops made an excellent impression on him. His Prussian companions from the Legation were smugly satisfied that the French were still less precise and stalwart.

After that journey Groener rounded out his broader experience with a longer tour of duty in Wuerttemberg. Now the paymaster's son was the operations officer of the Thirteenth Corps and the Duke of Wuerttemberg would read off Groener's reports as though they were his own. The simple young recruit had climbed to high levels. Now he was a major from the General Staff and the big man in the Corps. He plotted, led and lectured survey trips into the home countryside. He

organized a two-corps maneuver problem and helped to lay the
groundwork for an Imperial war game. As operations officer
he showed a preference for the timely withdrawal as a means
of regaining offensive mobility. The counter-attack, naturally,
was delivered into the side and rear of the advancing enemy.
Flanking action had come to dominate his strategic thinking.

Some verse at a Corps party probably gave some realistic
caricature of Groener's personality. In one skit he argued
against regional pride:

> "Schoen ists ueberall im Reiche,
> Jedes Land hat seinen Wert,
> Mag man dort die Weine preissen,
> Dorten mehr auch den Kaffee,
> Wir sind doch in einem einig:
> In der Liebe zur Armee."

Here was, in the parody of friends, a national German who
could appreciate traditional distinctions and yet also integrate
them in a united loyalty to nation and army. His life and career had developed in a new German spirit and he accepted it
as his highest social value. Local pride and class differences
were mere elements in this modern national unity and ego.

Another bit of verse had fun with his soldierly will and
daring:

> "Seht zum Beispiel Major Groener
> Welch ein kluger Mann, ein schoener!
> Wie ist ihm der Geist so vive
> Wie strotzt er von Initiative
> Schrecklich seinen Feinden allen
> Tut er nachts sie ueberfallen
> Ehe die sie noch bedacht
> Hat er sie schon umgebracht
> O der Grimme kennt kein Schonen
> Schlachtet Reiterdivisionen..."

The Prussian Groener was no longer a congenial "night light."
Now he was grimly aggressive and imaginatively daring. Maybe the slaughtered cavalry divisions even played on his technical accentuations. The respect of his staff seemed not to
lack friendliness but perhaps they were also struck somewhat
by his professional intensity. Life among the line units was

not that crisp and the returning Swabian from the General
Staff now had distinct Prussian markings. He could still re-
lax with his men but in the command tent he was a zealous,
systematic professional. At this stage of his life the Prussian
traits seemingly formed the profile of his personality.

In those last years before the war Groener also published
several essays which further illustrated his military passion.
In one article he envisioned the army as a sort of a national
school for the development of a proper Empire patriotism.
Here class and ideological differences could be fused in a
German "bond of comradeship." The intrinsic disciplinary
and competitive nature of army training would impregnate
young Germans against the pacifistic and anarchic lures of
socialism. The outward national unity could thus be given
deeper inward foundations. Of course such political orientation was to be managed with intelligence and subtlety, but
the tactful officer, comprehending social background and human psychology, could do much for the stability of the monarchy. The army might be more than a mere shield of the culture; it could help to consolidate and shape a modern Empire
patriotism.

Another Groener article encouraged the German soldiers
to serve as instructors and advisers in foreign countries.
Such cosmopolitan variety would enhance their individual
lives and better serve the new world ambitions of Germany.
The Empire would need men of international experience in the
years to come and the army should be alert to such future requirements. These military advisers could also be a wedge
for German business. There was a note of boredom in such
thoughts of foreign service, but always there was military and
national opportunism. For Groener the army was no dead tool
of the state. It was an active, formative, institutional force
in the cultivation of a stronger Germany.

A third article ascribed universal qualities of human nobility to the military life. It was entitled "Das Erhabene und
Schoene in der Kriegskunst." In it Groener asserted that war
was not just an animalistic struggle for right and might; it
had its own justice and virtue. War protected culture and,
like nature, it allowed manifold freedom within iron limits.
"The finest pages of history are those which describe how
spiritual strength overcame hostile destiny and surmounted

misfortune." Such words echoed the older Moltke and they supported the daring will of the Schlieffen Plan. They also represented a militant exploitation of older, purer German idealism. [17]

Groener and his colleagues found intellectual satisfaction in such military philosophy and they were quite ready for a martial clarification and rejuvenation. An exasperated old veteran like Colmar von der Goltz was tired of enervating peace and he wished Germany a good, hard fight so that the spartanlike Prussian virtues might be revived. Groener was not that direct or provincial but his spirit belonged in such company. War was a test and not a catastrophe. German prospects were grim but his army still trusted in its skill and power. Let the diplomats make their frustrated circles. The army had the will to cut Gordian knots and, armed with the Schlieffen Plan, Groener confidently awaited the "unavoidable military conflict" with his neighbors. He still regarded Europe as a competitive family, but the German stock was badly in need of a rally. He acclaimed the nerve of military action; he did not yet appreciate the higher nerve and ethic of diplomatic patience.

The vibrant Groener became Chief of the General Staff's railroad section in 1911 and thereafter Germany's lightning start would depend on his work. He thought his facilities could be improved and he immediately undertook an ambitious expansion program. The German rail net at that time included fourteen Rhine bridges, thirteen trunk lines into the important Rhine assembly area, four trunk lines along the Rhine, and four trunk lines across the Empire. Groener wanted five more Rhine bridges, seven more western trunk lines, and a special four-track through way from Hanover into western Germany. With improved locomotives, Groener worked to raise his traffic speed to twenty-five miles per hour and thereby cut three days from the mobilization timetable. German rail transportation was to fall stringently under his authority with the mobilization and military priorities not to be questioned, but his zone commanders did check with civic officials for possible emergency needs and special milk and food trains were somehow to be threaded into the mobilization schedule. Groener's section drilled incessantly on emergencies and improvisations. System and resourcefulness were considered to be the two basic requisites for a successful mobilization and subsequent supply race into northwestern France. [18]

Groener's projected improvements shot far over his budget allotments and he would get only one more Rhine bridge before the war started, and the other expansion requests were also postponed or rejected. But he still had an extensive quality system and its performance in 1914 more than satisfied the German expectation. In fact, its exceptional work and good fortune in that first summer campaign gave very dangerous substance to the extended flanking drive.

Budgetary restrictions held up Groener's improvement program and the General Staff was rather consistently vexed by such financial caution. The Empire lacked a modern tax structure as the confederate states resisted higher contributions and the Prussian nobility angrily checked efforts to levy a national property tax. Both of these elements opposed the idea of fiscal centralization and thus they obstructed the revenue needs of modern German power. The bourgeois delegates in the Reichstag were equally outraged by such conservative selfishness and money problems invariably triggered their sharpest criticisms of caste privilege and arrogance. Such bitter debate in the Reichstag periodically inflamed Empire feelings and exposed the serious ideological differences which still remained. The government became wary of these Reichstag explosions, and its officials often preferred to postpone or curtail requests for money rather than bring on more unpleasant exchange. Such debates seemed only to strengthen bourgeous pressures and further isolate conservative authority. Even a strong-willed Bismarck could remind his War Minister about such Reichstag irritability and ask him to shape his armament requests with some patience and shrewdness. Later German officials would be even more mindful of Reichstag turbulence.

The aristocratic army leaders found themselves in a very paradoxical position with regard to armament costs. Their request for more money invariably opened up the question of tax reform, thus exposing their class immunities to public review and risking Reichstag encroachment. The Chief of Staff generally did not regard such domestic ramifications because his job involved outward national security. He had to win battles against a foreign enemy and his strength had to

measure up to such opposition.  He asked for the money and
man power which he thought necessary to his international
assignment, but his requests had to clear through the War
Ministry and there were tailored to more complex specifications.  The War Minister had to fit his budget to the Empire's
income and gain the ratification of the Treasury.     Given
a  modest,  rather  inflexible revenue system, that Treasury office was stubbornly parsimonious.  The War Minister
also had to fight his budget through the suspicious Reichstag
and there he asked only for the money and man power which
he thought consonant with the internal stability of a Hohenzollern Germany. Excessive armament costs meant dangerous
argument and perhaps even tax reform. Excessive army growth
meant bourgeois and proletariat corruptions of an aristocratic,
patrimonial tradition.

The  War  Minister  wanted  to  neutralize the Reichstag
critics  with  deliberate,  clairvoyant  military progress.   He
could justify periodic requests for more armament money but
he could not annually tell the nation's delegates that the invincible German army was again in jeopardy.  His responsibility involved problems of fiscal and political attunement;
the Chief of Staff necessarily thought only of victory or defeat.  Schlieffen remarked that defeat would cost more than
timely armament.  The War Minister could only point to budget realities.  He was dubious about the rage des nombres
and he wondered sarcastically just how many corps the strategists needed to gain a sense of confidence. Schlieffen and
Moltke saw a circle of foes and knew only that they needed
more of everything. [19]

Such varied perspectives were understandable and illus-
trative of some balance of power in Empire fiscal matters.
Certainly the General Staff did not control finances as it did
strategy.   In fact there was a rather fatal lack of correlation
between the battle plan and the armament program. Schlieffen
and Moltke were allowed to prepare a campaign for which they
were denied the necessary resources.  Such lack of cohesion
in matters of higher policy was common to the Empire government.  All too many important officials were responsible only
to the Kaiser and their policies and decisions might be thoroughly divergent. And in the tangle of such personal government there was a basic estrangement between the authorities

and the people which also tended to deflect a full and frank discussion of the Empire's problems.   Groener thought the army's expanding twentieth century needs should be frankly explained to the people, and he was given to understand that the Reichstag appreciated Germany's foreign difficulties and was quite ready to boost armament expenditures.  After the second Moroccan crisis in 1911, an anxious Moltke suggested a yearly revision of the military budget, but the War Ministry preferred the more orderly pace of a five-year allocation (Quinquennat); it did not want to wrestle with the Reichstag on a yearly basis making it even more intimate with army affairs.

The military budget of 1911 allowed for modest technical modernization and even the extra armament bill in 1913 gave the General Staff only one of the three additional corps it asked for.   That reduction was decided on by the Kaiser and not by the Reichstag.   The War Ministry was afraid that a sudden, massive expansion would inundate the army's aristo-cratic breeding and the Kaiser agreed on more gradual growth. Generally speaking,  the government and the Reichstag were still in a wary bargaining relationship with one another, and the delegates were never taken into full confidence lest they intrude themselves even more into affairs of state.   Their constant reform stratagems were already bothersome enough.

As head of the military railroads, Groener appeared before this Reichstag budget committee to explain and defend some of the technical requests. He thought there was too much in-conclusive talk and not enough decisive consideration of Germany's actual military predicament.  He also represented the General Staff at special economic deliberations in the the Prussian Department of the Interior where he encountered comparable civilian indecision.  The soldier wanted a response to problems and not mere cogitation.  This was a crisp, con-fident Groener who epitomized the aggressive will and decisive intelligence of the General Staff, and he could not understand people who pondered without action.

The economic discussions in the Prussian Department of the Interior involved the question of Germany's ability to en-dure a longer war.   Industrial Germany imported over half of its raw materials, most of it by sea.   The certainty of an ef-fective British blockade was accepted and Admiral Tirpitz himself urged the government to study its economic position in the light of such maritime interdiction. It was Tirpitz who torpedoed the German chance for a reconciliation with Britain in the Haldane negotiations of 1912-1913. Like the Schlieffen Plan, his naval program guaranteed the very British opposition which could strangle Germany and negate General Staff strategy. Both Moltke and Tirpitz recognized the long-range implications of the British fleet, hewing to their respective Belgian and "risk" fleet projects despite opposition, and both were allowed to have their way by a deferential government and a kaleidoscopic Kaiser.

Groener's associates at these economic councils entertained some hope that America would insist on freedom of the sea in its trade with Europe and that Rotterdam might then serve as an air-pipe to the outside world. But others doubted such British leniency, especially if the German army were to operate through neutral lands. The eastern European hinterland offered some relief but even here rail facilities were inadequate and the Danube had never been used as a volume waterway. Even Balkan grain went to Germany by way of the sea. No matter how they approached the problem, the German economic experts saw no effective substitute for ocean trade. Germany's substantial agricultural self-sufficiency depended on large fodder imports for its animals. Without such imports, the animal stock would either decrease or get its fodder from acreage otherwise marked for human needs. The economic prospect for continental Germany was entirely frustrating and most of its experts estimated that a major war could be sustained only from nine to eighteen months.

Groener listened to some of these grim reports and he searched for an answer. Frederick the Great once set up a storage system. Would it be possible to bring in grain imports from Argentina and set up some sort of a food reserve to cushion the German need? But the council had considered and dropped that idea long before. Modern industrial production and consumption could not long be sustained from a static stock pile. The national expense would be doubled and the basic economic problem of war hardly improved. That sort of expense would be far better employed in a stronger armament program which might possibly bring about the needed quick victory. A few hoped for such a miracle. Others wondered about the fabled ability of trade to find its way through Findigkeit des Handels. Many trusted that the good sense of Europe would not permit a ruinous war to continue into self-destruction, and some had neither plan nor hope. All these men recognized the seriousness of the German position and yet their concern was hardly desperate. War was still only a theoretical possibility and the General Staff might even be able to do the job.

One warning by Moltke in those last years before the war was particularly prophetic:

> "The army command has the greatest interest in the avoidance of an economic crisis on the home front so that the soldiers may be heartened by the knowledge that the well-being of their families at home is secured. Economic collapse and hunger during a war would greatly heighten mass nervousness and invite the most unreliable elements of the people to forcefully push their revolutionary aims. The morale of the troops, which is the most important and most sensitive instrument of victory, would suffer heavy damage if unsteadiness would spread about at home."[20]

The army knew what home front discontent could mean to its effort and to the state. But Moltke did not allow such somber thoughts to change his war plan. In fact he now was prepared to grab Liege on the fourth day of mobilization and practically eliminate the chance of British neutrality. German strategists understood their problem and they sailed right into it. The storm would prove too much for them.

Such militant will and national determination expressed the character of German policy before 1914. This was the exaggerated ego and voluntarism of the Empire which Meinecke judged to be so much responsible for its collapse. The German interest was to be asserted by bold action rather than patient circumspection. A peaceful resolution of Europe's tensions at that time, however, did not rest solely on German behavior or intent. Different German action would not necessarily have dispelled problems which entwined many states and multiple factors. One can only say that the Empire's emphatic style and bold military leadership very substantially reduced chances for a diplomatic adjustment.

Groener was one of these German activists.  He and his friends in the General Staff were men of character and intelligence who were allowed to direct national strategy with their narrow campaign logic.  Groener even visualized the army as an orientation school for proper national patriotism.  He wanted military leadership to be a primary force in national life and policy.  Only when World War I exposed the limitations of mere force and will did he come to understand that the army could more intelligently serve the nation as a responsive arm rather than as a directing instinct.

Chapter Three

## THE NAIVE SOLDIER

In 1913 the Kaiser and his people celebrated the twenty-fifth anniversary of his regime. It had been an era of great economic growth, political ferment and cultural dispersion. Patriots and critics, materialists and aesthetes crossed swords freely on a gradual decline toward jingo creeds and profane values. The minority regime still held the reins with firmness and trust even though the ride was generally rough. International pitfalls threatened constantly and the political underbrush at home was growing ever thornier. The social Democrats, for example, were now the largest party in the Reichstag, but the restless subjects also knew how to count their national blessings and they were prepared to defend their Fatherland. Its problems could be attacked freely and its orderly way of life undergirded the vibrations of social and political struggle.

German life was energetic, disciplined, argumentative, ambitious and impulsive... not exactly misrepresented by its Kaiser. British statesman Eyre Crowe could laud its civilizing accomplishments and also be on the alert against its dynamic unpredictability. And Germany's own Max Weber once phrased his picture of the young Kaiser and Empire, "One has the impression of sitting in a high-speed train but worrying whether the next switch is properly set." The rational Weber was very much exasperated with such a national predicament, but his analogy probably expressed the Empire's sense of daring thrill and action under the last Hohenzollern King and Kaiser. [1]

William wanted to expand his Empire into a world power and he was determined to maintain the outmoded citadel of Prussian authority at home. Therein lay his two primary objectives and the paradoxical tension of his regime. His world

52

ambitions required a solid domestic foundation which was impossible if he insisted on patrimonial privilege and leadership. Industrial Germany furnished the impetus and muscle for such world ambitions, but it also created the bourgeois and proletariat opposition to Prussian feudal leadership. Many wanted him to recognize the new pillars of modern German power and adjust the monarchy to the liberal and democratic fashions of a changed society, but William thought himself destined and sufficiently adroit to manage the new Germany in the older Prussian manner. He surveyed the Empire from his Prussian citadel and he recognized its expansive energy, but his comprehension of such modern force remained purely mechanical. He was unable and unwilling to dignify the social and political spirit of the new German world and he could only respond to its egalitarian demands with instinctive junker alarm. His sovereignty was based on God's grace and the army's loyalty, not to be infringed on by rebellious subjects. He wanted loyal citizens who knew how to express their freedom respectfully, within the limits of the Bismarck constitution. His concept of Imperial responsibility was once strikingly illustrated by a marginal comment, "An outstanding election slogan would be that the Kaiser is responsible for the nation's security and it can demand of him that his measures guarantee its safety. He who votes for this is for the Empire. He who votes against it is against the Empire." William wanted the nation to have the right to confirm his absolute authority.

    The right arm of such Imperial authority was, of course, the army. "We belong together," he could tell his military paladins. "We are born for one another and we shall eternally stand together, whether God's will gives us peace or storm." This army stood beyond the dimension of the regular German government and was exclusively at the Kaiser's disposal. It gave reality to his assumptions of absolutism and the two actually did stand together above the state. The young Kaiser could tell his generals that Bismarck was dismissed because he refused the crown military obedience. Twenty-three years older, in 1913, he offended the political sensitivities of virtually the entire nation in supporting military authority and arrogance in Alsace. His archaic, class-conscious absolutism was anchored by his exclusive military command and in the esprit de corps with his fraternal war lords. They heard his innermost feelings and represented his ultimate strength. His civilian officials recognized this primacy of the military and they seldom ventured to contest with the men in uniform. It was highly commensurate with Hohenzollern tradition when the Kaiser fled to his army during the last days of revolution and defeat in 1918. Groener's pronounced judgment that the troops would no longer respond to royal will cut through the innermost cord of the Hohenzollern dynasty. [2]

Many intelligent and sensitive Germans could regard the Hohenzollern system with tolerant affection. Friedrich Meinecke still thought that such experienced Prussian power was necessary to the further progress and elevation of the German interest. He was uneasy about the alienation of labor and the crass materialism of German politics, but he hoped that such tensions and corruptions could gradually be resolved with national wisdom and civility. Meinecke delivered a speech in honor of the Kaiser's twenty-fifth anniversary in which he praised the personal leadership of William as a treasured aspect of German life. He and his countrymen insisted on the personification of government. They would "go through fire" with the Kaiser and follow him up "steep paths to the beclouded heights of (their) future." For Meinecke the worlds of Goethe and Bismarck were in some effective conjunction under the Empire. He trusted in a continuing refinement and integration of such a blend and he honored the Hohenzollern part in such German growth. [3]

A less sentimental man like Max Weber could only explode at the Empire's twentieth century behavior. National unification and industrialization had prepared Germany for world expansion. Indeed it could not maintain its European power unless economic and military buttress positions were added in the colonial world. Population needs alone required expansion even if Germany were politically content to be a quiet Switzerland among the giants, but then the unification would have been a "boyish stunt," without sense or purpose. Expansion into the colonial world was also vital to the future measure of personal freedom. The open, defenseless regions of the world were being claimed by the big powers. Soon all would belong to resolute states and each people would subsequently be forced to contract within their own territory.

Those nations with more land would be able to enjoy economic living room and affiliated individual freedoms. Thus it now behooved the Germans to get as large a slice of the globe as they could.

Weber's grim imperialism was certainly not out of step with Germany's new world policy, but he was bitter with both Bismarck and William II for their reactionary obstruction of intelligent German growth. Bismarck restricted Germany's colonial interests and his continental diplomacy would disregard alliances of global import. At home he effectively crippled the political parties and thus denied the nation sound training and evolution in modern government. He even stultified the development of an experienced diplomatic corps since he arrogated all important work unto himself and his son. When he finally abdicated, Germany stood without colonial help, without domestic political experience and even without a national bureaucracy capable of managing a modern power. The great junker autocrat simply stopped the process of national co-ordination at a point convenient to his diplomatic and class interests. The Empire was left administratively and spiritually dissonant, and it lacked the inward organization and solidarity necessary to successful expansion. And the impulsive, offensive antics of young William only worsened the problem by pulling this unsettled Empire into global projects.

The junkers instinctively grasped the dangers of further national integration, for the new material and psychological needs of Germany were not suited to their patriarchal way of life. The city people wanted a voice in public affairs in order to express their will and serve their needs. Their constant push for more rights threatened to inundate the patrimonial junker world, and the alarmed, unbending nobility fought back from behind their constitutional dikes. Weber respected their contribution to the national cause and he appreciated their fight for survival. He wrote,

> "It is the tragic fate of the German East that by its great contribution to the nation it also dug the grave for its own social organization. ... It was not narrowness of view but a certain awareness of what must come, when outstanding men in

Prussia, on up to the highest level, resisted as-
similation into the greater unity of the Empire."

But the die was cast by history and now they had to be swept
aside in the interest of German evolution. The new age owed
them nothing. But to Weber's exasperation, the German nation remained by the side of its reactionary Kaiser. Efficient
bureaucratic maturity was delayed and the patriarchial founders
still had their giant by the collar. This frustrated Weber's
concept of German progress and he was bitter toward both his
government and his countrymen, but he was fiercely loyal to
the German state as such and angry only because its greater
global opportunity was not being rationally exploited. [4]

Max Weber espoused a cold Staatsraeson which was
committed to the national interest in whatever situation and
under any political form propitious to the age. More sentimental patriots like Meinecke and Groener were rooted more
firmly in the Empire tradition, but they too would come to
recognize that junker authority could no longer be permitted
to bridle the nation. Their thought on this matter was prompted
by wartime lessons and the exigencies of defeat. And their
constant loyalty to the German state, as empire or republic,
also reflected the supra-ideological national feeling of Max
Weber. Meinecke himself described his group of wartime
acquaintances, which included Groener and Weber, as modern
German politiques who sought to tone down factional interests
and accentuate necessities of state. [5]

The jubilee year in 1913 witnessed Germany in a moment
of difficulty and hesitation. The tensions and limits of the
hierarchic, federal Empire were in distressing evidence.
Diplomacy accepted the guidelines of the military and allowed
that very British enmity to be fixed which could throttle German power. The Reichstag was excluded from the basic decisions of government and the Social Democrats, its largest
party, were still distrusted as revolutionary enemies of the
state. The Kaiser regarded that Reichstag as a rival, not a
partner, in the management of German life. The Empire was
in dangerous international straits but little was done to organize it internally. Suffrage and tax inequities still reflected
an inward dissonance of right and spirit. The business blocs,
the bureaucratic agencies and the federal states all pulled

for themselves first and tended to regard unification as an
opportunity rather than a responsibility. Certainly the much
celebrated German efficiency was not present on the higher
levels of national life and policy.

The Germans were beginning to wonder where it would
all lead. And yet they still felt their nation to be in ascen-
sion and somehow capable of resolving its problems. Hindenburg probably expressed more than mere military outlook
when he said in his memoirs, "Yet greater than our worry was
our confidence." But the Empire's fall was not far off and
its confident strength would slowly be exhausted. Then an
earlier Meinecke prophecy would come to pass, when he
wrote about the democratic tide in 1907,

> "There will come a time when this flood, perhaps
> driven by the winds of a world political crisis,
> will tear down the present artificial barriers. Then
> all will depend on whether the new ground of lib-
> eral and industrial Germany will have the political
> and national steadiness to substitute for that which
> is levelled."[6]

The junker-industrial relationship in Germany throws
light on the conflicting historical forces which engaged with
one another in that Empire. As a Swabian bourgeois and as
a railroad officer in the General Staff, Groener was affiliated
with both contesting worlds. He represented a personal syn-
thesis, as it were, of the Prussian-German union and its
disjointment under the pressures of World War I also disrupted
his own life harmony. Confronted with irreconcilable alternatives in 1918, he chose modern German continuity and left
the Prussian tradition to its fate. That decision seared his
life but he courageously abided by its sense in his service
to the successor Weimar state. The naive soldier became a
politique who urged and demonstrated the subordination of
faction and sentiment to higher national considerations.

War finally came to Europe and Germany in the summer
of 1914. Now their competitive principles of life might again
be exercised in ultimate match play, and the roar of the
crowds in every capital gave strange enthusiasm to the feared
contest. Many decades of nervous diplomatic maneuvering
created a tense irritation which exploded in the moment of

decision. Undoubtedly Germany's internal frustrations also
contributed to the patriotic outburst in that country. It was
a moment of family reconciliation in crisis.

As the Austro-Serbian crisis in the Balkans developed,
Groener was one of the many German leaders who dispersed
with the Kaiser for the summer holidays—but only after William made his "blank check" commitment of support to the
Hapsburg state. Then the excessive ultimatum to Serbia ensued and Europe's alliance chains began to fasten each nation to its post. Collective security also meant collective
sensitivity and the storm clouds gathered over all the major
powers. Groener was on his way to Switzerland, but he delayed in Stuttgart as the ultimatum to Serbia was rejected.
He was ordered back to Berlin on July 26 where he and his
colleagues quietly watched the storm develop. Their long
awaited test was now under way and they were not afraid
Groener's timetables and marching orders lay ready and l
declined their last-minute review. He wanted no nervo
excitement in his office. He smoked his cigars and wait
for the diplomats to end their bit. When he was asked abo
his attitude toward mobilization, he gave the laconic rep
"better tomorrow than the day after tomorrow." He was read
to go.

Less tranquil, and with good reason, was Chief of Staff
Moltke. He was too sensitive and nervous to confront such
a moment of destiny with stoical resolve, and his opening
battle plan was misleading and daring enough to excite most
any man. He planned an immediate stab for Liege on the
third night after the beginning of mobilization. This opening coup was so carefully guarded that the Cologne railway
district would receive its transportation assignment for that
special assault project only after the mobilization began.
German control of Liege was considered to be a first decisive
requirement and Moltke had this surprise operation very much
on his mind as the diplomats fought for time. He wanted
clarity and a quick decision. He was even afraid that the
French might beat him into Belgium, already working that
danger into the diplomatic prelude to his campaign plan. On
July 26 he drew up the ultimatum which said that French troop
movements toward Namur forced Germany to move into Belgium for its own security. This was the very note which the

German government then presented in Brussels on August 2.
The French army alert had barely begun as Moltke wrote his
plot reflecting his nervous military fear and his slick understanding of international diplomacy.[7]

Moltke almost did collapse when, a few hours after mobilization began, the Kaiser ordered him to hold up the western
operation and prepare for an eastern war only. A misleading
telegram from the German ambassador in London gave some
hope of British and French neutrality. But Moltke had no full
assembly plan for the east and he would have had to reverse
his western mobilization. He excitedly told the Kaiser that
such a turn-about would leave them with a chaotic mob of
armed and hungry soldiers. Such lurid fears notwithstanding,
William sensed a saving opportunity and he ordered Moltke
to hold up the first step into Luxembourg. Moltke went to
his room and sobbed, contacting nobody. Then the hopeful
note from London was revealed to be a misunderstanding and
the Kaiser told his Chief of Staff, " now you can do what you
want," whereupon Moltke rushed his troops into Luxembourg.

Groener was the man who would have been asked to turn
those troops around to the east, although he knew nothing of
the incident until later. He always agreed with Moltke that
such neutrality in the west would have merely postponed
French and British participation at the expense of the German
chance for victory. But, said the railroad expert, such a
mobilization switch was not a technical impossibility. The
armies were not yet being assembled and the Groener staff
was well versed in the unexpected. The unavoidable initial
confusion could have been worked out.[8] The machinery of
war did entwine the strategist in a powerful chain of automatic
preparation, but man still pushed the buttons and mobilization
was not an inexorable commitment to war. More decisive
was the fear and opportunism of men and nations, who feared
the power of others and thus sought to get in the first crippling blow. The Schlieffen Plan was really based on insecurity, finally even desperation.

Groener's railway section received its alert on July 28.
Bridges and depots in the border provinces were placed under
guard. Troops needed for immediate border or service duties
were recalled to their home stations. On July 29 the entire
army was ordered to assemble at the base garrisons, and

railway guards were posted throughout the Empire. On July 30 the fleet was alerted and supply trains were dispatched to the northern ports. The mobilization of the rail system itself began on July 31 with the declaration that a "threat of war" existed. The peacetime schedule continued, but special military trains were pressed into it. Freight traffic in the eastern and western border provinces ceased and railroad cars were collected in the interior. Alsace-Lorraine alone was cleared of almost five thousand freight cars. Germans crowded into railway stations all over Europe and flooded into the homeland. The German passenger service was tested to the limit and, in effect, momentarily conditioned for the military assignment to follow. Full mobilization was ordered on August 1 and all German railroad transportation passed into the hands of Colonel Groener. Now he and his crew suddenly found themselves to be the mainspring of the German war machine. The gamble for a quick victory in France depended first of all on an instantaneous delivery of the armies to the frontier.

On the evening of the third mobilization day, all civilian traffic stopped and the military schedule of twenty miles per hour went into effect. Within two weeks a force of almost two million men was assembled along the western frontier. Five hundred and fifty troop trains daily crossed the Rhine. Every ten minutes a train moved over the northern Hohenzollern bridge at Cologne. Not one of more than three thousand railway substations checked back for instructions from Berlin. The only traffic knot was quickly unravelled as the daily four-hour pause gave officials their chance to straighten out congestion. Only one troop train suffered more than a slight delay. The cavalry unloaded to give chase to some automobiles thought to be the fabled "gold cars", speeding bullion to Russia. Even the railway schedule could not completely govern such fantastic excitement. [9]

Groener was a picture of ease and confidence. His mobilization was a faultless demonstration of General Staff efficiency. Even a quip about a blown Rhine bridge was lightly deflected. Call me when there are two down, he joked happily. He was ready to divert an entire army to the right bank of the Rhine. By August 12 an army of over three million men was assembled and Groener joined the Kaiser's party as it headed for Coblenz to direct the campaign in the west. The Kaiser had already given his railroad chief a silent hand of thanks and the railway section of the General Staff garnered the first Imperial citation. Groener was suddenly an admired and exemplary figure and German faith in the General Staff was apparently being justified.

A German assault unit moved toward Liege on the night of August 3-4. Armored trains with motorized and cavalry support moved out to secure and begin repair of the crucial rail connection between Aachen and Liege. Belgian demolition orders were issued that same night but they were late and poorly executed. Track destruction was ineffectual and the damage to small bridges, switches, and station facilities was not crippling. The numerous bridges, viaducts and tunnels along this twenty-five mile defile were seized relatively intact and a golden chance to spike the German advance was lost. The rail entry into Belgium was secured and the first gamble of the campaign succeeded. The Belgians apparently lacked thorough demolition plans and they were further surprised by such quick action at the very outset of the German mobilization. [10] On August 17 three armies of the flanking wing began their advance across Belgium. Their progress was rapid, as the defenders side-stepped into Antwerp or withdrew toward the south and Allied help. German tactical progress quickly cracked through resistance points at Namur and Maubeuge, and in early September it was curling down on Paris. Then came the French stand along the Marne and the collapse of the German venture.

The German command planned to extend its Aachen-Liege supply stem along two basic routes. The outside First army would run its line to the southwest, from Liege to Brussels toward Cambrai. The inside Second and Third armies intended to work their line to the south, from Liege to Namur toward St. Quentin. Additional cross-army supply help was also expected by way of Luxembourg-Libramont-Namur and later in the drive by way of Metz-Sedan-Laon. These important lateral arteries (rocades) would give systematic circulation and emergency responsiveness to right flank traffic. The Germans did not expect to capture these railroads undamaged and yet they figured to reconstruct a functional skeletal framework in step with the advancing front. Groener trusted in the element of surprise, the skill of his crew and the density of the Belgian and French rail systems, which promised to allow for numerous alternate routes. At least track would have to be activated for ammunition supply. The troops would have to live off the land as much as they could.

Groener's railway progress was both fortuitous and difficult. The outside line quickly reached Cambrai and by early September it seemed that the First army was well launched toward Paris and the lower Seine. Again the Belgians missed vital demolition opportunities to the west and even northern France allowed sound track to fall into enemy hands. The French did not expect the invading flank to extend beyond the Meuse and last minute demolition efforts lacked sufficient engineering personnel, but they did severely block up the Namur gateway and all significant routes to the south between the Sambre and Meuse rivers. Liege was not connected with Namur until September 2, and even then supply service into northeastern France continued to depend on small-gauge improvisation track and lengthening truck hauls. Also the important tangent lines from Luxembourg and Metz were not effectively tied into the right flank supply zone until after the Battle of the Marne. [11]

Thus only one of the four projected supply lines was in satisfactory contact with the fighting front as the September test neared. The Second and Third armies were expected to furnish the inner muscle of the sweep on Paris. They encountered not only better demolition work but also stiffening resistance and both looked apprehensively at their faltering rail support and straining truck service. It was Buelow of the Second army who first warned, on August 25, that the advance would stop unless the railroads caught up. And he was just beginning the descent into France, with its greater track destruction. The long cogitated supply problems of a rapidly advancing flank were now becoming grim reality.

Groener's men were turning in a resourceful pressure performance but their skill and luck also had limits. Long, key bridges were down at Namur and Hirson, and the entire supply needs for the Second and Third armies had to go the western way around, by way of Brussels and Cambrai. Those bridges would not be repaired until the late Fall and the Buelow complaint would not be satisfied in time for the Marne decision.

The rudimentary occupation net was not immediately ready to convey both soldiers and equipment but Groener frequently had to alternate the two. A corps from Schleswig-Holstein was threaded through to the Antwerp front. A show-piece heavy artillery batallion from Austria-Hungary was given exceptional track clearance, for German precision was on display.

In late August two corps were shipped east from Namur and in early September an entire army was rushed up from Lorraine. The Aachen-Liege run was chronically late and restrictive in peace-time. Now it labored under the supply needs of three armies and intermittent troop-train disruptions. And a loud cry for ammunition would go out in September as the opening campaign climaxed and these modern armies suddenly showed their enormous firing needs. Needless to say, it was not Groener who sponsored such criss-cross troop movements at a time when a systematic supply push was both necessary and difficult. Moltke's complicated maneuvers foolishly taxed transportation facilities and the relative simplicity of Schlieffen's power drive now seemed even more sensible to Groener.

There were many other problems as well. The German military railway service was short on man power and specialist officers. Cramped training facilities denied them experience with standard track operation and major construction work. These were shortcomings which simply had to be corrected in the field. Beyond the frontier, strange track and left-handed traffic slowed up the trains, as did curves, grades, and track bedding considered to be below German safety standards. Even the Belgian coal fell through the German grates and everywhere civilians cut track and wire, or stormed trains and stations. Nor was Groener plagued only by such enemy "rascality". His own troop commanders did not easily respond to railroad regulations. Many held up trains for their unloading convenience, then housed troops in the empty cars. Some units hoarded their own supply stocks and almost immediately attached themselves to railhead service. Others stole entire trains from one another and hid these so effectively that they were not found until after the Marne. Some unloaded ammunition trains were later turned up in areas where the need had been greatest, and most vocal. Not a few trains lacked sufficient ticketing and were lost in the shuffle. The anxious commanders thought track repair meant supply and they were slow to realize that signals, sidetracks, loading ramps, and water tanks were also necessary to service. Groener drove his men and snapped at the armies. He warned them from the very start to comply with railroad regulations or jeopardize the operation. He was working for systematic circulation in lieu of advance depots and his traffic patterns required absolute co-operation. [12]

Such initial friction between front and rear echelon reflected natural tenseness and adjustment. It also indicated a hair-line supply gamble and latent crisis. Despite great German luck and energy, the railheads were losing contact with the fighting front and Groener wanted the right flank to pause and tighten up along the French-Belgian border. Consistent extension, even with a day's pause, seemed more important than disjointed haste. But Moltke pushed his armies on, working for the necessary rout and afraid that delay might enable the defenders to settle behind formidable river barriers.

In the last week of August, Moltke made three decisions which Groener considered fatal to the operation. He withdrew two corps from the right flank and sent them to the east. He launched a second offensive along the Toul-Epinal front denying his Belgian armies timely reinforcement from the south. And, on August 30, he turned the German right flank inside of Paris and gave up the deeper envelopment. With each of these orders, Moltke violated basic principles of the Schlieffen Plan. Massive right-flank strength was never assembled as Moltke moved his units with amazing flights of strategy. His strategic reserve of six divisions were early sent to the Lorraine front. Then two corps were lifted out of Belgium, far from effective rail transportation and critical to right-flank success. Apparently Ludendorff did not even insist on reinforcements from the west; he was confident of holding on with what he had. But if help was to be sent, then the Lorraine front did have more available manpower and it had direct rail contact with the eastern theatre. Its units would mill around inconsequentially as the Belgian drive began to fade for lack of manpower.

The Toul-Epinal assault, ordered by Moltke on August 27, also wrinkled Groener's brow. The whole Belgian operation was motivated by the German unwillingness to grind through this formidable French defensive position. Now the extended Belgian flank, the head-strong center under the Crown Prince and the Lorraine troops would all join in a composite maneuver involving a flanking envelopment, a penetration assault and a general push. Moltke lost control of his armies, and strategic clarity, by the end of August. Defeat at the Marne was not a military miracle; it was a smart French counter-attack into the side of a fading German drive. [13]

By the end of August, Groener saw that the French army was still very much in the field and that the German drive was thinning out, but he still wanted that right flank to move out toward the southwest. Maybe its extension would still serve to take the French off balance. Also Arras and Amiens were key transportation points and they could furnish flank security against the coast. A transportation line over Brussels-Cambrai-Amiens would allow him to build up that weakening outside flank and increase its pressure. Groener walked around headquarters rotating his elbow to the outside, but Moltke pulled his armies to the east of Paris and the Schlieffen Plan was dead.

The right flank army leaders reported that they did not have the strength to continue toward the west of Paris. They were worried about their open Channel flank and began to ask for reserve strength. Moltke accepted their assessment and, on September 2, he ordered his right flank to pass northeast of Paris and try to pinch off French units between that city and the Mosel. German momentum, force and cohesion were gone and the curling right flank was now itself exposed to envelopment out of Paris and Amiens.

In contracting toward the southeast, the German flanking armies were pulling ever farther away from their one good supply line over Cambrai. The scene of major combat action was shifting into very difficult transportation areas. The military railroad map for early September, 1914, showed a great transportation pocket between Hirson, Laon, Reims, and Sedan. This was the very supply zone of the Second and Third armies as they worked along the Marne. The small end railheads were jammed and all trucking units were exhausted. Some combat elements were one hundred miles beyond their rail supply and, according to one of Groener's aides, "it was

momentarily out of the question for the railroads to catch
up...." [14] The right wing had not received, nor required,
massive supply during the war of movement, but now it was
worn thin and logistically insecure for the decisive flurry
which followed.

The French commander in Paris watched the German flank
curl by and expose its side. Reinforcements poured into the
Parisian front as the French rail system demonstrated its own
flexible capacities. Joffre then launched his decisive counter-
attack on September 6. A two-pronged operation drew the
German wing apart and opened it up for a dangerous Allied
wedge. The entire German right flank was in danger of being
cut off or badly maimed. Its armies fought viciously and Joffre
did not fully exploit his opportunity, but he had splintered
the German offensive and thwarted the enemy's bid for a quick
victory. The entire German strategy, military and diplomatic,
had been subordinated to that knock-out effort. [15]

Moltke and his headquarters had only sporadic impres-
sions of the decisive action along the Marne. Far to the rear,
in Luxembourg City, he and his staff dragged along with one
telegraph receiving set. His armies were instructed infre-
quently by radio but a direct exchange of information was
never possible. The critically engaged First army did not receive a single command from Headquarters between September 6 and 9, as it was fighting for its life. Control of the
operation was gone and Headquarters could only wait to see
how their armies had fared. As Groener wrote to his wife,
"This waiting period until the decision has fallen is a ruinous
test of nerves. We see, hear and feel nothing of all these
battles. The infrequent telegrams which we receive only
serve to heighten the tension." The great plan ended in a
strategic vacuum.

Moltke stood in helpless anguish, on the verge of collapse. "It goes badly," he told his diary on September 9.
[The battles in front of Paris] will be decided against us. We
cannot avoid suffocating in the battle against east and west.
How different it was as we opened the campaign so brilliantly
a few weeks ago. Now comes the bitter disappointment. And
we will have to pay for everything which has been destroyed!"
Groener flexed well under defeat though disillusioned by the
mediocrity of German leadership. All went well until Schlieffen

was "forgotton or laid aside; then the big victories were finished." The great Leuthen had not been struck and an entire
generation of military thought was frustrated. Only the striking victory at Tannenberg in the east veiled the German failure and cushioned the shock. A stolid, old Hindenburg
remarked that the young men would now have to drop Schlieffen's
legacy and do some of their own thinking. [16]

Groener's stubborn faith in the Schlieffen Plan merits
some assessment. Failure along the Marne began Germany's
twentieth century decline and of course it stirred fervent controversy. Many tacticians argued that the field was won and
then foolishly abandoned. Others ruefully conceded that the
right flank lacked decisive force and was bound to fall short
of complete victory, north or south of the Marne. Studious
strategists, like Generals Kuhl and Groener, reaffirmed the
logic of the flanking move and they found fault with Moltke's
instrumentation. Military historians like Hans Delbrueck and
Gerhard Ritter have scored the entire war plan as a political
and strategic mistake of the greatest import. Its aggressive
bid for victory clearly exceeded Germany's military capacity
and it ensured world hostility. Its bold Machiavellianism
introduced the twentieth century problem of a heedless German power and behavior. Greater military restraint in 1914
could hardly have damaged the German interest as much. A
mobile defense along the western frontiers was not impossible
and it would have confronted France and Britain with difficult
problems of strategy and diplomacy.

It seems clear that the Marne was not lost because of
supply shortage. The right flank armies had enough to fight
with and they withdrew in order to seal their splintered front.
Ammunition needs were frantic but apparently not decisive. It
is possible that supply uncertainties helped to break the
German nerve, although no commander made such an admission. But all three right-flank armies had already expressed
their supply concern and they were working even farther away
from their railheads. It is probable that graver deficiencies
would have developed had these armies held their ground and
prolonged the engagement. It was the retreat to the Aisne
which again gave them a sound logistical foundation and again
stabilized the German line.

All the right flank armies were tired, weakened and in-

secure. . . by their own admission. They were at the point of
envelopment but they did not have the strength to follow
through. They still flailed dangerously but without positive
co-ordination. The Channel flank was dangerously exposed
and reserves were not within immediate reach. Even the official German history of the war wondered whether its army,
"because of its difficult supply situation, . . . was in a position
to exploit any possible success" along the Marne. A maximal
extension of the invading force was reached and a reorganiz-
ing pause was necessary. Then the trench war would have
developed along the Marne, rather than the Aisne, and the
Schlieffen gamble for quick victory would have been equally
frustrated. [17]

Seemingly the great flanking effort did lack conclusive
man power, logistical carry and tactical co-ordination. Did
the fault lie in the plan itself or in its implementation?

Groener pointed an accusing finger at Moltke. Success
depended on decisive man power and deliberate, relentless
pressure. The German government never fulfilled Schlieffen's
specifications and Moltke modified the plan. But, thought
Groener, even the drive of 1914 could have been pursued to
victory. The French attacked in Lorraine, left the Belgian
door wide open and were not prepared for German action west
of the Meuse. The enveloping action, with sound rail support over Liege-Brussels-Cambrai, was confronted with no
significant resistance. Amiens lay within German reach and
it would have given even greater strength to the German position. The German flank was hooking the defense and it
needed only to maintain its direction to the southwest to ensure complete envelopment. Somehow Paris would have been
reduced, had it been invested, and it would have surrendered
enough booty to help propel a further advance should such be
necessary.

Man power was critical to such a sweep but it too was
within reach. The six reserve divisions in Germany should
have been sent to Belgium, not Lorraine. The two corps at
Namur should have been left in the line. The Lorraine army
should have been brought north in time and systematically
marched in from Aachen. The trains for its transportation
stood ready, but they were used too late. An entire German
army was on the rails as the German fate was sealed north of

Paris. Even then, decisive strength might still have been generated along the Marne had the whole German line angled toward the northwest and brought its force to bear toward Paris.

Groener readily admitted that his occupation rail net could not initially carry both men and supplies. Schlieffen never expected the troops to ride into France. Deep echelon strength depended only on timely, persistent man power consignments to the Belgian front. This Moltke did not do and herein lay his fundamental error. Groener's assessment had its own share of logic, hypothesis, and oversight. He argued that the weight of the German drive should have been kept to the outside, where the flanking grip could keep the defense off balance and where volume supply was possible. Certainly German man power was not well committed in that opening campaign and Moltke did not exploit his right flank potential. The Belgian venture hardly seemed justifiable in the light of such meandering interest. But such uncertainty notwithstanding, the possibility of a quick victory seemed nonetheless slight. The supply columns were losing contact and the German drive was running out of breath.

Groener's own supply study once pointed up the vital need for motorization and that deficiency still existed in 1914. Motor trucks were perhaps more critical to that opening campaign than man power. Harness teams were too slow and the motorized connecting rod between the railroad and the combat unit was not enough for the need of the moment. Groener's comment that the reduction of the Parisian fortress could somehow be effected, even without a full investment force, also lacked sobriety and proof. Schlieffen and the older Moltke knew what that great complex could soak up, and Paris could hardly be discounted by an inspired wave of the hand. And if Paris should fall, what about Britain with its constricting navy and broad world influence? Like Schlieffen, railroad chief Groener thought primarily of the continental fight. The British army could be locked into the Channel ports. Maybe the General Staff unconsciously expected diplomatic negotiation with Britain once the French army was defeated. But its written thought shows no such broader conjecture and the German military's wartime attitude toward truce proposals hardly reflected any earlier calculation along such lines.

One can only conclude that the strategic views of the General Staff actually stopped at the water line.

Any mechanical appraisal of the Schlieffen Plan necessarily lies in the realm of hypothesis. It was Moltke's fate to accept, modify, and mismanage the strategic concept of his forerunner. His instincts were strange to its radical daring and no one knows whether Schlieffen would have done any better. Perhaps he also would have learned that will power does not prevail over all, nor does it validate a theory. His plan was admittedly not feasible in 1906 and it still lacked strategic soundness in 1914. Groener agreed that it depended on the effective seizure of the Belgian and French railroads. The Germans were lucky at Liege and in northern France. Their inside flanking elements then passed through heavy demolition work and soon encountered serious supply hindrances. How sound was a plan which gambled on the enemy to miss his demolition assignments? If supply success depended on motorized help, how feasible was the plan in 1906, or even 1914? It was generally recognized that the plan required a perfect opening performance. How realistic was it to assume the faultless co-ordination of new masses and new techniques after forty-five years of peace?

Schlieffen portrayed the modern Alexander at a broad desk, in comfortable quarters, serviced constantly by telephone, telegraph, motorcycle, automobile, and airplane, but his army either was not taught, or it did not absorb, the new technical lessons and it failed the practical examination in 1914. In fact such facilities and techniques were yet more visionary than actual. Moltke quailed in a youngster's school bench as the German right flank fought its decisive action. There were not enough railroad men, not enough trucks, not enough telephones, not enough telegraph stations, not even enough Liaison officers. Moltke should have dispatched communications officer Hentsch on an entirely different mission. The modern Alexanders could not convert theory into practice overnight, as the Schlieffen Plan apparently expected them to do.

Groener could maintain that no German unit lost any engagement because of supply deficiencies. This was true enough but it hardly covered prospects at the Marne or beyond. The German front retracted before supply scarcities were exposed and even the critics of this retreat confessed that the armies could not have pushed farther without man power and supply refurbishment. The entire campaign required spectacular good fortune and a perfect performance by one and all, but it only came close and its failure forfeited all subsequent strategy.

Groener's railroads were not able to save the Marne but they did sustain the German line along the Aisne. Groener wanted the new Chief of Staff, Falkenhayn, to detach his right flank and rebuild his striking power near such rail points as Mons and Namur. From such a rear base the German force might coil again for a second major effort. But Falkenhayn was afraid that his own flank might be turned and he raced the Allies to the sea. Groener's railroads were used to string out that line, rather than build up a new offensive force. The long front was spread-eagled from Switzerland to the Channel and it lacked both defensive agility and offensive concentration. The impasse of trench war was already evident.

A final, wearing push was launched at Ypres but piecemeal troop commitments robbed this action of decisive force and it developed into a murderous attrition grind. The "flaming enthusiasm" of Germany's university youth was not enough to overcome the artillery barrage, the machine gun, and the entrenched foe. "We are nailed fast again," wrote Groener in October, 1914. "The long, long line has operative immobility." The failure at Ypres confirmed the defeat at the Marne. The French campaign could not be ended quickly and the German leaders now had to face the feared realities of a two-front war and a British blockade.

Groener was no longer the ebullient optimist of August, but he still thought that the army could resolve its problem and he wanted no intrusion from the diplomats. The strategy of the naive soldiers had failed but they were yet at the head of a great army and still bent on a martial course of action. Groener would cling to such militaristic logic, reflected in his diary, letters, and memoranda, until 1916.

August was a month of great pride and bold-soldier talk. Groener told his wife about the high railroad accomplishment, his great authority, and his position of favor with the Kaiser. The latter was "very friendly" to him and paid him "great compliments." Everything moved according to plan and it seemed to be "the greatest moment that Divine Providence has ever conferred on the life of the German people." Even Moltke's slimmer <u>bataillon carre</u> in Belgium was effectively forcing the quick victory and "the spirit of the blessed Schlieffen" accompanied them. The French were declared to be "on the hip" as early as August 23, and Groener reassured his wife that the war in the west was already won. "I am and have been of this firm conviction from that moment when our railroad and approach march succeeded in brilliant fashion." Belgian rascality and British interference were mere annoyances. They would put every British prisoner to bed with a Russian and teach him not to impose such a barbaric ally on the Germans again.

The "iron dice" were now rolling and it was no time for hesitation or sentiment. "In order to achieve great things in war," he wrote, "one cannot be hard enough. . . . One should always aim for completeness, never be content with half measures; the golden mean is not suited for war." Fortunately the General Staff was not in charge of German destiny and it would correct the failures of the diplomats. It would do a "thorough job" and give the German people peace for the next hundred years. The Chancellor and his group seemed to think that war was a "philosophic concept" and probably inclined toward a convenient peace. But "that was out of the question" and the General Staff would take care of "Herr von Bethmann and the other fools of the Foreign Office." It would root out this "humanitarian nonsense." Fortunately the Kaiser was very much on their side and no longer listened to the "weaklings." The German future required hardness, not sentimentality. Let the enemy expire by the "hundreds of thousands;" as long as the Germans were strengthened thereby.

By September, Groener's military scrutiny was coming back into focus. Despite the many proclaimed victories, there were few prisoners in evidence. On August 28 the Germans were only five days' march from Paris but Groener was already worried about its defensive strength. His journal expressed concern about the open Channel flank and the exposed supply line running along that coast. One day before the Marne, Groener conceded to himself that "we don't have the man power" to force the Parisian front and sufficiently buttress the Belgian position. On September 6 he wondered how long

the campaign would last and he began to hope for a big victory
in the east.   Maybe it would help to break French resistance.
When the Marne results finally trickled through, it was clear
that the bid had failed and that "much hard work" loomed a-
head.   The enemy was "so numerous" and the German people
would simply have to work their way through this great crisis.
Now he could be slightly annoyed by the brassy hero talk
which still prevailed at the Kaiser's table.  The German people
might be better served by a frank enlightenment of their
situation. [18]

Groener was never happy with the deceptive style of the
German war communiques.   It merely created a sense of security and convenience at home, and the nation was not properly attuned to the grim challenge at hand.   Of course, such
propaganda techniques involved more than narrow military will
or strident Hohenzollern fashion.  Conservative authority and
reform fears also helped to motivate the deception of the public.   Victory prospects would tend to justify the established
German regime;  indications of difficulty might stir up public
dissatisfaction.   The Prussian autocracy was now bedeviled
with the fruits of its proud and exclusive authority.   It could
not trust the German people with grim news and so it maintained a posture of heroic duty and invincibility.   In England
the people were one with the government and there was no
fear of realistic danger and intensive public sacrifice.   The
historical breach between the Prussian authorities and the
people obstructed such a sober, mature exchange of frankness
and effort in the Empire.   The hierarchic state was not well
geared for the total mobilization necessary for modern war.
High sacrifice was expected of all Germans and in such a
democratic situation the presence of constitutional inequali-
ties was regarded by most as intrinsically immoral.

Evasive about reforms, the regime was yet intent on sustaining the united esprit of August, 1914.  Thus it spoke of
duty and Fatherland,  invincibility and victory.  The Hohenzollern system seemed well protected and well justified by
such thoughts. It sensed that anything short of victory would
place the government under irresistible reform pressure.[19]
Thus the eternal victory promises, the tenacious annexation
plans, and the unwillingness to settle for a compromise peace.
In the end it was just as unwilling to admit defeat.  Of course,

such public deception was rather decisive for the shock and
anger of October and November, 1918, when defeat could no
longer be concealed and the culprit dynasty no longer maintained.

By the end of 1914 Groener was rather resigned to a tenacious struggle and perhaps only a partial victory.  Britain
could obviously not be brought to heel by the German army
and this war might see only an expansion of the German position on the continent.   Then "many new soldiers" would be
needed for the final reckoning with Britain. Groener began to
see his war in terms of a Punic struggle. He was already beginning to improve the German rail connection with the Belgian
system for the next war to come.   And it was "so nice" to be
able to "command such work to be done without much talk and
correspondence, whereas in peace it took seven years of ink"
and negotiation to get one Rhine bridge. The railroad colonel
was already building for the next war and apparently Belgium
was to remain important to German strategy.  A geopolitical
asset like that was certainly not to be surrendered after victory.

It was at a Christmas party in 1914 that a rather heady
Groener expounded more publicly on the future control of the
Belgian railroads.  Falkenhayn was apparently impressed and
two months later he asked Groener to put his ideas in writing.
The army was interested in maintaining an occupation force in
postwar Belgium and Groener's respected technical views
might help to influence the German course of action.  Thus
he could participate in the widespread "memorandum assault"
for expansion which characterized German politics in the
Spring of 1915.

Groener's memorandum declared that the railroads were
the "necessary foundation" for the armed might of a nation.
Modern strategy involved the assembly and mobility of mass
armies and no plan should evolve without full railroad considerations.  Alsace and Lorraine were taken in order to buttress German strength along the upper Rhine. Now the German
march into Belgium "still had to squeeze itself laboriously
past the Dutch province of Limburg." Since this war was not
the last of the series, the German army must "gain space" in
order to set itself for the next. Belgium must be occupied so
that the Ruhr industrial area might be shielded and France

held in a permanent flanking grip.

The future political status of Belgium did not concern Groener. He spoke only for a strong occupation force and direct German military control of the Belgian railroads. Groener expected Belgian resentment and he was prepared to bridle it. He wanted no interference from German civilian bureaucrats who might "allow Belgian interests to step to the forefront" or even try to "find the soul of the Belgian people." With such a net at its disposal, the German army could run through maneuver and railroad problems at will. It could finance its own occupation costs and perhaps even return some surplus to the Empire. The military railway service could ramify its organization and training without cost to the German state. Belgium would be seriously hurt, of course, by the loss of its railroads. "But since the interests of German business do not allow the economic independence of Belgium to be sustained, military and business logic here join." Groener stressed railroad and military desiderata, but he was also shrewd enough to suggest revenue benefits for the Empire and market expansion for German business.

This memorandum well reflected Groener's militaristic view of life. Belgium and Alsace-Lorraine were mere positions in Germany's strategic alignment. Their own civic ego and happiness was entirely irrelevant. Belgium was appraised for its significance to the Schlieffen Plan of the future and for the opportunity it offered to Groener's military railway section. There, presumably under his able direction, it would gain control of an entire national work. What an improvement that would be over the paltry facilities of prewar days. His memorandum reflected personal, professional, and national ambitions. Very decidedly, he was yet a naive soldier whose political comprehension was controlled by the strategic outlook. He saw the world from the perspective of military history, but he did not have enough foresight to note in his journal that the Belgian project was a bit premature. [20]

Groener's Belgian memorandum conceded that a complete German victory in the west no longer seemed possible. The Empire could only strengthen its European position and wait for the next round. Like many other Germans, Groener turned his eyes to the east where large victories and deep expansion were still possible. In 1915 Naumann's Mitteleuropa scored

the biggest publishing hit since Bismarck's memoirs. Here
lay a natural German interest after failure in the west signalled
the restriction of maritime expansion. "The imperialistic effort is finished," wrote Naumann; "left is withdrawal to the
continental position, to the Bismarckian tradition, though
transformed and deepened." The world was consolidating into gigantic American, British, and Russian blocks. Could
smaller, but talented, central Europe assert itself among such
global giants? That was the "fundamental question" and the
alternate opportunity for German influence and leadership.
Naumann thought of his Mitteleuropa as a group of states with
a common future, related in an economic confederation under
German leadership. His friend, Max Weber, was more interested in a straight, unsentimental German hegemony. The
generals and the professional patriots talked of direct annexations or frontier territories. [21]

Groener had no particular program for eastern Europe. He
only saw that the German armies could win in the east and
there acquire an economic hinterland which could cushion the
blockade and strengthen the German position for the years to
come. He had no fixed territorial objectives, but he and his
Staff colleagues were "not at all happy" with Bethmann-
Hollweg's idea that the new Germany should stretch out to the
Meuse, Niemen, and Narew rivers. The Chancellor was much
too moderate, thought Groener, and apparently inclined to forfeit improvements earned by the blood of thousands. He could
only hope that the German people would "rise up against such
weakly views." Groener's political world still consisted primarily of pedantic bureaucrats and dilatory diplomats. They
allowed Germany to slip into its dilemma and they must not be
permitted to hold up thorough military corrections. [22]

In Germany, the year 1915 was one of steady strength,
inconclusive victories and gradual concern. The west front
held firm but several German drives in the east stopped short
of damaging victory. Falkenhayn was content to stab the
Russian giant off balance and build up for his great assault on
France. His outward poise and confidence had done much to
steady the German headquarters after the Marne, but he lacked
strategic breadth and he did not understand how to exploit the
very considerable strength which the German army still had.
As Groener commented irritably in his diary, "He never has a

great operative idea, no inspired soul, always only the small, immediate goal." Groener wanted major eastern campaigns, to drive deeply toward Vilna in the north or Kiev in the south. He respected Ludendorff and Hindenburg, who seemed to understand strategic sweep and mobility. They did not hesitate to withdraw for the moment or strike for the deep target. They gave real substance to Germany's new eastern dreams even though denied conclusive help by Falkenhayn.

Groener's railroads functioned impressively in the frequent troop shuttles between east and west, but such piecemeal switching was more spectacular than effective. Within half a year he dispatched sizeable consignments to Poland, East Prussia, the Carpathians, and Serbia, but a real power push was nowhere launched and in the east it could neutralize an entire front. Groener basked in the headlines for his railroad heroics but he was thoroughly exasperated by such continued fragmentation. Such mistakes had cost Germany the French campaign and created the two-front dilemma. Now they continued to plague German strategy on a front where significant victories were still possible. Each operation required its own due time and concentration and it should be geared for a complete campaign victory. This also was a Schlieffen principle which fell into disregard.

In that eastern whirlpool the German generals were also annoyed by the kaleidoscopic political considerations. Bethmann-Hollweg was worried by early Austro-Hungarian discouragement and Falkenhayn was persuaded to send troops for a late winter attack into Galicia. It bogged down in heavy Carpathian snows. The Gorlice operation in the Spring was undertaken in part to display German power and check the Italian and Rumanian drift toward the Allies. Its success was not carried through and German attention then shifted quickly to Serbia. The supply route to Turkey needed clearing and Rumania merited a further demonstration of German capacities. In the north Ludendorff was denied break-through strength for his Masurian Lakes campaign for fear of exposing West Prussia to possible Russian harassment. German headquarters in the east buzzed constantly with plans for a new Polish state under German supervision. Even in the west, political considerations jostled the men in uniform as Germany gave up its submarine war in deference to the American protest.

Groener was not happy with such meekness nor did he like
the repeated intrusion of political thought into military decisions. Victory was the key to national satisfaction and the
soldiers should be left to do their job. If only they could
"neutralize all the diplomats," the war would be over much
sooner.

Groener's grumbling in 1915 retained an aggressive edge
and yet it was not without pensive hesitation and insight. He
regretted that his prestige and leadership had blossomed so
late in life. Now his verve was somewhat restrained, "for
one does not become wiser with age, rather plum-soft, which
is then called experience." He was sure that his prewar views
on strategy were all confirmed, but he had not expected the
German-front to stretch out in such long, inoperative lines,
"with which no great success can be attained." The diplomats
were a nuisance, but he also knew that Italy's decision for
war and Rumania's independent manner reflected significant
foreign assessment of the German prospect.

Notable civilian acquaintances were growing dubious
about their country's situation. Historian Hans Delbrueck told
Groener they might do well to settle for status quo ante bellum.
Friends in the Food Office were beginning to see black and
Groener probably remembered that prewar estimates for German
self-sufficiency ranged from nine to eighteen months. In the
early months of the year he told Falkenhayn to build a modern
defensive fortification line from Metz to Ostende and the Chief
of Staff was amused. After a summer of Balkan and eastern
meandering, Groener was even more guarded about the military
prospect. Neither his government nor his superiors seemed
to have a clear idea as to how to proceed and what to aim for.

Groener dropped one particularly intuitive comment during those months of frustration as he noted that the "notewor-
thy aspect of this war" seemed to be that the "correct military
decision so often steps into the background of other considerations." This war was strangely complex for the General
Staff which wanted to fight and win on the field of battle. It
did not fully understand that modern strategy might be better
implemented by diplomatic and economic leverage. General
Ludwig Beck later observed that his fellow officers were not
prepared to reckon with strategy different from their own.
They did not see that the instruments of modern military power

no longer lay with the field operation and the tactical unit. Even Groener first understood his railroads primarily as a tactical instrument. When the military effort failed, his duties then involved him in domestic transportation which showed him the mounting economic strain on beleaguered Germany. He sat on coal and food committees; his trains delivered the physical needs of the nation. In the Fall of 1915 his office organized the badly needed "cereal trains" from Rumania into central Europe, which relieved public apprehension somewhat and again glamorized his public image.

Groener was the resourceful specialist who could thread Germany through its two-front difficulties, but he was hardly happy with such temporary solutions; they could only postpone the developing constriction of the Empire. "The foe sits at the longer lever," he admitted to his diary, "and it was our job to prevent a war of attrition (Ermattungskrieg) from wearing us down." Certainly his "hooray" naivete was gone and he was being forced to grapple with the economic conditions of war.

Groener's Christmas letter in 1915 well reflected the pensive mood of an experienced and concerned soldier. He wrote to his wife,

> "Let us hope that we may again celebrate next year in peace. When one regards the war situation, one cannot help but think of Frederick the Great and the Seven Years War. And if the present war does not last exactly seven years, we must yet prepare ourselves for a third Christmas in the field. Let it be and come as it will, we will just have to stick it out."

Now he too was ready to agree with Hans Delbrueck that Germany could be content with status quo ante bellum. He was no longer willing to risk American intervention with submarine activity. He disagreed with those who thought Britain might be willing to negotiate on terms favorable to Germany. That well-positioned foe was not going to "let loose" and "submit themselves to our terms." He was even dubious about Falkenhayn's coming assault on Verdun and France. A drive toward Odessa seemed much more rewarding and sensible to Groener. He now understood the complex risk and nature of

total war, and he was no longer a naive soldier. As he said
in his memoirs, "The time in which I should be carried away
by unfounded hopes was past. I began to regard our situation
very soberly and, ... it was very serious. Great caution appeared to be in order." The war was now clearly a desperate
struggle for survival in which the Empire might well be happy
to settle for its old frontier and its old way of life. [23]

Chapter Four

## THE POLITICAL SOLDIER

Germany's geo-political restrictions were recognized before the war and discounted. They were ominously realized
after the failure of the opening campaign. General Seeckt
described the Empire's position as that of a "beleaguered citadel," which could launch sallies but which lacked the final
force to break the siege. The first attempt was the strongest;
each succeeding strike against Allied constriction must necessarily be weaker. In 1914 the German army neglected to concentrate decisively at the vital point. Thereafter it lacked
the leisure to do so within its concentric fronts. The General
Staff was thus consigned to the very kind of mobile defense
which it had feared and sought to avoid. "That is the fruit of
the evil deed," sighed Groener to his diary as he watched the
German army pursue its fragmentary defensive strategy in
1915. That was the "fate" which they could "no longer evade"
unless miraculous good fortune might yet "fall in their lap."[1]

Groener and his own section aides had discussed Germany's strategic problem and generally agreed that the defensive advantages in trench war were to be heeded. They favored
defense in the west and bold offensive drives in the east, but
Falkenhayn kept his eye on the west. Russia was too vast and
the Balkans too peripheral for war-ending action in the east.
He would wear down the French army, which he considered to
be the "sword of England," and simultaneously strike at the
blockade with unrestricted submarine action. He decided to
apply relentless pressure at the focal point of Verdun and
bleed out the French army. A break-through was not even
planned for. Perhaps the British army would then be tempted

into starting an incautious relief offensive.    Verdun could
thus start out as an attrition campaign against the French and
loosen up the enemy front for a series of terminal maneuvers.

Groener was not excited by the idea but he gave assurance
that a formidable concentration of men and fire power could
be mustered by the rail system.  He did not appreciate an assault which was not planned to break through, and he saw no
logic in Falkenhayn's intent to bleed out the French while at
the same time inviting American intervention with submarine
war.   But hope sprang eternal and on the eve of the offensive
he wrote almost prayerfully, "Maybe the fortunes of war will
come to our aid once more and give us a situation which is
made for fast action—I hope we will know how to move then."
His journal then marked the tension and critical delay of the
pending assault.

February 12.  "Rain...opening bombardment postponed."

February 13.  "Night...starry heavens...morning...misty
Knobelsdorff hesitates to shoot! Rain the entire day! If Verdun
does not start soon a surprise is doubtful.

February 14.  "Rain .... It is impossible that the attack
against Verdun can move in such weather."

February 15.  "Rain, nothing but rain.  Verdun continues
to be postponed and deserters from the Fifth or some other
Corps.  It is hardly likely that the French are still uncertain."

February 16.  "It continues to rain.  Knobelsdorf and the
Crown Prince have no weather luck....The rain has let up some
in the afternoon, the skies are clearing. —in Berlin a preacher
has supposedly asked God's Grace from the pulpit for our
pending offense!!"

February 17.  "The weather is clearing.... The French are
excited about Artois .... No talk of Verdun....A war-ending
success in the west is impossible.  Odessa.  A blue sky is
pushing through the clouds—Kaiser-weather is on its way."

February 20.  "The past night we had a full moon, today
the sky is bright. If this weather holds for a few days we can
finally start before Verdun."

February 21.  "Fine weather!  We have been shooting on
Verdun since this morning.  General Falkenhayn and several
of my staff have gone up.  God grant that the attack will succeed and that losses will not be too heavy."

February 22.  "The Temps in Paris informed its readers

that the Germans might attack Verdun. It reassured them that the fortress was strong. If the Germans really wanted to attack there, they could be could be assured of a rousing welcome."

February 23. "Our artillery barrage is quite intense; it is a tremendous spectacle .... One could only see the giant clouds of our shells .... Soon the entire mass of our artillery fire was united on the town of Brabant—the town disappeared in black and gray explosion clouds so that the houses and church could be seen only now and then. ... In the meantime it began to snow."

The great assault was under way and a new chapter in mass war was opened. The scene was more horrible than impressive to the men up front, who crouched stupefied in their forward posts and waited to spring up in dutiful sacrifice. More than ever before, the individual soldier had become a mere mathematical figure in the new strategy of attrition

The front line made "nice progress" for a few days. "Fort Douamont has been stormed. ... Bravo," wrote Groener. But the enemy stiffened quickly and hundreds of trucks brought in reinforcements. Fort Douamont did not fall and by the end of the month the German attack was in need of a pause. The long rains softened up the clay roads and supply was a harassing problem. The artillery added to the difficulties by making the first displacement away from the major ammunition dumps, in violation of the planned pattern. Falkenhayn brought in more heavy artillery from Belgium and later he stripped the armaments from such fortification points as Metz and Diedenhofen. German strength was being truly expended and the French packed their line to meet the attack head-on. Losses were huge and both armies were strained to the breaking point. One German corps, which was withdrawn for shipment to another front, virtually ran to its trains. Falkenhayn truly took the "bull by the horns" but he wore himself out in the struggle. The French maintained their will to continue and they could better afford the losses than the Germans. They were supported by world resources, not surrounded by them.

Douamont finally fell and, on March 9, the Germans reported the capture of the other key bastion, Fort Vaux. Groener was both happy and wary. "If the fort stays in our hands, then it is the second breach which has been laid into the fortress—

and its effect on the Parisians—in case they are informed—
will not miss its mark." But German enthusiasm was foiled
again and the sour diarist had to admit that "Fort Vaux was
recovered by the French as we trumpeted out our victory fan-
fare." By the middle of March it was clear that Verdun would
not fall. Even the systematic Falkenhayn hesitated and he
pondered an alternate offensive in Flanders, but his strength
was already gathered at Verdun and he decided to "bleed out"
the French. His request for unrestricted submarine action had
also been fended off by Bethmann-Hollweg, and his great offensive against the west was checked within three weeks.
The grind and the losses continued but the German bid for a
decision in France was painfully tied up. [2]

Groener detached his hopes from the struggle with a mo-
rose threat that the Allies had better hang on to Verdun "because if we ever get it we shall never give it up. If we want
the Briey ore basin then we must also have Verdun." It was
a mere departing volley, for he was certainly more discouraged
than aroused by the costly failure. Again the German strategy
seemed pedestrian and he was only afraid that its problems
would be compounded by unrestricted submarine warfare. A
mere fifty submarines could not cripple the British, who would
confiscate more German tonnage in neutral ports than they
would lose to the submarines. The navy had done enough to
complicate the German assignment and he was not impressed
with the "theatrical" Tirpitz. Certainly American manpower
should not be brought into the war for a submarine action which
seemed to be more spectacular than effective. Let the navy
be quiet and assemble a fleet of several hundred submarines.
Then the question of their use might be re-opened.

Groener received his relief from Verdun in May and June,
and he once again toured his eastern stations. There the
Austro-Hungarians were reeling under Russian pressure but
Groener was not upset. A few setbacks would restore a proper
degree to the ally, who was overly flattered by recent success
in Italy. The east was now a tactical breeze for the German
forces and Groener could cockily predict that they "would restore things to order." He had no respect for the Hapsburg
army and when the Bulgarians refused to place themselves
under its command, he could only comment flatly, "they are
probably right." When a chastened Falkenhayn consulted with

Conrad and for once promised quick help, Groener again could not refrain his sarcasm, "Both strategists departed again this evening, apparently pleased to find themselves sponsors of the same idea, which is supposed to happen very seldom among strategists." He was sour with the world and beginning to regard its problems with tough dispassion. There would still be intermittent flights of hope, but his spirit was gradually building its shell as the disappointments became more and more suggestive of a basic trend.

On his way back to the west, Groener stopped off in Berlin to attend Moltke's funeral. Like Bethmann-Hollweg, the former Chief of Staff was a tragic figure in the decline of the Empire.[3] Both were intelligent men of culture, sensitive to German problems, but neither was gifted enough to control his strategic assignment, and each was considerably responsible for the dilatory strategy on the home and fighting front. Both were forced to withdraw in failure. Moltke sought a balanced offensive and stumbled his way into diffuse fragmentation. Bethmann was looking for a "diagonal" policy at home which could find the line of compromise between the various German parties. He finally satisfied no group and was pushed aside for the unilateral leadership of the High Command.

Groener was a frequent visitor in Berlin as he made his inspection trips from front to front. There he could see his family, participate in various transportation conclaves and continue acquaintances in one of Berlin's foremost war societies, Die Mitwoch Gesellschaft. There he came in contact with Walther Rathenau, Ernst Troeltsch, Hans Delbrueck, and Friedrich Meinecke, who undoubtedly influenced his views on war and peace. These men were moderates in matters of war annexations and by 1916 they accepted the necessity of suffrage reform in Prussia. Delbrueck and Troeltsch were among the first to speak up for a peace negotiation without expansion. With Rathenau they thought that Germany's best postwar opportunity lay in a friendly relationship with Britain and a more restrained colonial program.

Meinecke had moments of a slight expansion fever, but by 1916 he thoroughly opposed annexation and argued for more traditional European restraint and sophistication.[4] He and Groener promenaded with one another and the general was

exposed to new ideals of European civility and careful <u>Staats-</u>
<u>raeson.</u> This meant that German power must understand its
physical means and its cultural responsibilities. The life of
a neighboring state and the conscience of the German citizenry
were to be respected. Groener's agile spirit expanded in such
company and he began to discern the deeper implications of
the war and the broader problems of the nation. After Verdun
the stability, survival, and future of the German state would
concern him much more than isolated campaign strategies.

The Berlin visits also brought Groener contact with home-
front morale. In January, 1915, a friend in the Food Office
told him the nation could feed itself for one more year. The
"cereal trains" from Rumania at the end of that year testified
to the approximate accuracy of his prediction. Such basic
staples as grain, cotton, and copper were becoming scarce
and prices rose as supply fell. But private enterprise still
filled the shop windows with nonessential products and the
federal states in the south kept their food supply to themselves.
Those with money bought good food in the black market and
those without grew hungry on their shrinking rations. Many
still hoped that the General Staff could save the day. But
another pole of sentiment formed around the socialists, who
were growing increasingly suspicious of bald victory promises
and impossible annexationist demands. They resumed their
criticism of the government and a policy of competitive self-
interest within the nation.

A victory peace seemed clearly unlikely and even of sin-
ister import to their democratic program. The junker monarchy
would then be more self-righteously entrenched than ever.
And a negotiated peace was hardly possible as long as German
leaders entertained their expansion claims, especially in the
west. Their suspicions were not groundless, for the German
conservatives, junker and conservative, were very much conscious of a relationship between annexations and status quo
reaction at home. They planned to disarm public discontent
with imperialistic ornaments and patriotic exaltation.

The crisis-galvanized Empire of 1914 was beginning to
pull apart again along its class and regional seams. It had
not substantiated that initial surge of unity with any tangible
symbols of a new relationship between government and nation.
The physical needs of the citizenry were not given impartial,

decisive attention, and the comradeship of a nation in arms was not honored by any official recognition of basic constitutional rights. The Hohenzollern Empire had the nerve to ask mass sacrifice for its system of privilege. Under Bethmann-Hollweg's representation it cogitated the ethics and tactics of political reform. But the military emergency after Verdun brought Ludendorff and Hindenburg to the western front, who understood the industrial importance of the home front and who would ask for even greater domestic sacrifice and discipline. Their will to manage the home front economy was logical enough in the narrow military sense, but labor and the Reichstag were hardly in a mood to consign even more of German life into the hands of two such junkers incarnate. The home front wanted constitutional reform in exchange for any new concentration of effort. It would be confronted, and dominated, by a high-handed Ludendorff who thought that every German must be a soldier under his command. This was his concept of military responsibility for victory.

The Tannenberg heroes were brought west in response to German weakness after Verdun. The Allies launched their own major offensive with Russian pressure in Galicia and a smashing British push along the Somme. Now Falkenhayn faced an enemy application of "brutal force." British artillery hammered down the German batteries and literally blew up the defensive line. The German front began to erode away and the first signs of exhaustion and anxiety became visible among the men in grey. This was the great <u>Materialschlacht</u> which impressed on the German army the tremendous Allied edge in resources. Equipment, firepower, and food simply abounded among the khaki-clad and suddenly the German soldier felt himself to be in a doomed cause.

Ernest Juenger drew a memorable portrait of the new German soldier, his face shadowed by the steel helmet, set in grim, weary, dispassionate lines. He fought with professional skill and forgotten purpose. Even back at Headquarters, the face of Falkenhayn assumed the weary set of his troops. His confidence was gone and he was suddenly a hesitant old man—even his own aides recognized that he must be replaced —but the Kaiser liked him and for a while resisted any change. Rather typically, four days before accepting Falkenhayn's resignation, William said to him, "we will stay together until the war's end." The Kaiser was not at all eager for the her-alded and confident pair from the east. He knew what every-body else knew: that the strong-willed Ludendorff was hard to live with.[5]

The new High Command received authority in a moment of German military crisis. They were the Tannenberg victors and they had cudgelled the Russians with unremitting consis-tency in Poland and Lithuania. The fatherly old Hindenburg and his aggressive executive had caught and actively culti-vated the fancy of the German patriots. There was German steadfastness and nerve combined in one harmonious command unit. Hindenburg and Ludendorff carried the shaken German hopes and their recommendations would be hard to oppose. They represented the final military effort and were able to un-derstand, and impose, themselves as the final, absolute guardians of the Empire.

Groener was one of those who believed that the eastern pair should be given a chance on the major front. He did not like Ludendorff's brusque egotism and radical will, but he had high regard for his military talents. Ludendorff knew how to concentrate an operation and give it bold, decisive lines. Groener had frequently spoken for his man power and supply needs when Falkenhayn considered reinforcements for the eastern front. Ludendorff was often a thorn in Groener's side on matters of supply and transportation. He was imperious about asking for rail support and quick about destroying track. He pressed constantly for more supply although he was often negligent about its care and distribution. He was a deficit organizer who scrounged for tomorrow's battle and trusted to victory to solve subsequent problems. In short, he was a stereotype militarist who thought primarily in terms of the tactical need and expected the nation to serve the military. As early as 1915, Groener jotted into his journal, "How will it all turn out with him. Already I see him sitting on a very high throne as Chief of the General Staff." And when Luden-dorff finally did come west, a friend remarked to Groener that his forcing style might well completely exhaust Germany and even endanger the dynasty.

The initial action of the new commanding pair typified their style and spirit. The Reichstag was assured that every-thing was under control even though the Somme strain had the

German army wobbly. In early September they held a war council with the government leaders. The men in uniform were in favor of unrestricted submarine war and Admiral Holtzendorf predicted that Britain's will to fight could be broken before the end of that year. Bethmann-Hollweg opposed with the thought that a negotiated peace through President Wilson might still be possible. Ludendorff admitted that he would like to finish the Rumanian campaign first whereupon the pliable Bethmann agreed that submarine action was a matter of proper military timing. Ludendorff saw his opening. He too thought that it was a decision for the High Command and he asked the Chancellor to stress this point to the Reichstag. He regarded that body as nothing more than a rubber stamp and he was absolutely brazen in his abuse of its function and intelligence. When the Chancellor later protested that he had the constitutional authority to decide on submarine war, Ludendorff reminded him of the earlier understanding and insisted that he was responsible for victory. [6]

The long fumbling and disrespected leaders of the Empire government were now caged with a tiger and Bethmann's verbal meditations would be ruthlessly falsified and exploited. And he lacked the tradition of office, or combative sense of responsibility, to subordinate the generals. The long Prussian deference to the men in uniform, often controlled by men of wisdom, now gave an embattled Germany into the hands of a willful hasardeur. His verve was not yet blunted by failure or by the frightful attrition of war in the west, and he would force a final German effort.

Groener recovered some of his buoyancy with the coming of Ludendorff even though he recognized the unpleasantries and risk involved. Maybe he could restore German military security in the west and give new verve to the war effort. Groener was not initially impressed with Hindenburg who sagely disclosed that his main worry about unrestricted submarine war concerned the reaction "of Holland and Denmark." And a baffled Groener wrote in his diary, "apparently he does not think of America." But he himself could still say things which did not exactly correspond with Germany's military predicament. His own peace program was recorded in a conversation he had in August, 1916, in the midst of the Somme crisis. He told a friend,

"A Russian policy in the Bismarckian fashion.... No
self-reliant Poland.... In the west bring back the
King of Belgium,  but keep Belgium in a dependent
tie with Germany—keep the railroads, make the
Belgians intermediaries for our industry. Win over
Holland.  Social Democracy at home,  directed by
the government.  We cannot get through without
state socialism,  therefore grab hold rather than
wait."

This did not sound much like status quo ante bellum and obviously such talk represented one of Groener's happier moments in an anxious summer. The image of a negotiated peace
changed constantly and perhaps this August conversation was
attuned to the outlook under a new High Command.  Groener
did not like the prospects of German moderation and he entertained more ambitious hopes until the very last summer, but
they became ever more exceptional to a basic trend of pessimism.

These diplomatic notions were not strange to an admirer
of Bismarck and Schlieffen.  Holland and Belgium were again
appreciated for flanking purposes. A Bismarckian relationship
with Russia expressed the interest of the General Staff. Satellite plans for eastern Europe seemed tangible enough since
the German army already was asserting itself from the Baltic
to the Black Sea. The new feature in the Groener outlook was
his acceptance of the need for a domestic realignment.  Maybe
he had learned from his Berlin friends that the junker foundations of Frederick the Great could no longer satisfy modern
needs and sensitivities. An industrial monarchy of the twentieth century rested on mass support and mass self-respect.
The Kaiser should recognize such new foundations and associate his authority with a new state socialism.  In such a
democratic monarchy,  the tradition and discipline of the old
state might best be aligned with the welfare and ego of the
modern public.[7]

Groener was beginning to think of Empire evolution. The
German interest obviously rested on the energy of its people
and now the crown was expected to adjust itself to such new
national factors, but in his military position, he was still entwined with colleagues who would rather cripple the nation

than change the governing system. Such talk of a socialistic monarchy was confined to private conversation although it probably drifted to other ears as well. Groener's Swabian instincts and flexibility were coming alive again as the national dilemma deepened and he began to work with the imperious Ludendorff. The new order was rather clique-conscious and resented by many of the troop commanders, but the High Command esteemed his ability and he was the only officer not in the operations section who was invited to eat at the table with Hindenburg and Ludendorff. Such high favor was fatal to Groener's life, for it would soon pull him out of his railroad sovereignty and make him a satellite to the coming strong man.

Ludendorff knew that the war in the west involved a strategy of supply and he sent Groener on a tour of the front to study army needs after the battle of the Somme. The General Staff was working out a call for total mobilization which was to be known as the Hindenburg program, and Groener was a natural choice to direct such a production assignment. His transportation experience and reputation seemed valuable to any military supervision of the domestic war effort. Industry and government had failed to organize an efficient war economy and now the army was eager to intercede.

Groener's background included varied contacts with the civilian economy. His railroad work involved considerable supply and assistance from German industry and he was familiar with the transportation needs of the domestic society. All traffic depended on his clearance and priorities and he knew about the foodstuff and raw material problems of every area. Before the war he had participated in the vexing supply discussions of the Prussian government and he represented the army in the delayed effort to set up a co-ordinated War Food Office (Kriegsernaehrungsamt) in the Spring of 1916. The Empire stumbled badly over its factions and states as no one wanted to be subjected to a regimented economy. The southern states kept their food and the Prussian junkers adhered to their own cultivation habits in defiance of government crop regulations. The northern cities had no particular assets and they were gradually reduced to subsistance nourishment levels. The socialists clamored for an Empire rationing program but had to settle for a maze of separate and ineffective food agencies. There were offices for potatoes, fruits and vegetables, sugar, fats, fish and eggs.

This bureaucratic tangle was further tightened in 1915 by a poor harvest which ranged from 15 to 35 per cent lower than normal. Relief shipments from Rumania helped some in the winter of 1915-1916, but Austria-Hungary soaked up most of the Balkan grain. The fears and predictions of the prewar councils were now materializing. Germany simply did not have the position or the resources for a longer war. The munition factories were beginning to request higher rations for their workers and there was a sprinkling of strikes and food riots in the summer of 1916. The Somme crisis further accentuated German need and Allied wealth. [8]

The food problem seemed most immediate in the Spring of 1916 and the Empire government assayed another bureaucratic formation. It planned a national Food Office in which representatives of various German groups could appraise and direct commodity distribution. Falkenhayn earmarked Groener as the army delegate to such a council and the latter was agreeable, provided he might simultaneously command his railway troops— his professional anchor. The railroads gave him leverage in any economic issue and identified him as a man of means and influence. He went to Berlin in the middle of May to present his ideas on food supply to Bethmann-Hollweg. He asked that one military authority be given charge of all domestic, occupied, and front-line supply needs. Such a supply czar must be free of all regional military intrusion.

Groener had experience with rear echelon impediments and he wanted a free, authoritative hand. Undoubtedly he had himself in mind for the job. How else was his own transportation sovereignty to be reconciled with that of such a supply czar? Groener saw only civilian bankruptcy and he thought the public was ready for, and in need of, more efficient military leadership. His concept of leadership was more consultative and fair-minded than the brassy and clannish manner of Ludendorff. The latter commanded from a pedestal of uniformed, junker authority. Groener addressed himself to the national emergency as an impatient, talented organizer who sought productive discipline from every German, and he regarded every last working man as an equal fellow citizen, but war was no time for democratic discussion or bureaucratic indecision.

Groener's concept was not accepted, for the War Ministry

did not care to see the General Staff intrude itself so deeply into home front affairs. That command zone belonged properly to the War Ministry. Thus a Multi-member Food Office was created in which Groener was only one of seven and president Batocki of East Prussia was its executive head. Groener had with his transportation knowledge and instrument expected to be the key man. But before the original group of seven ever began its assignment, the Reichstag camel also stuck its nose into the tent. Soon there were eleven in that group and another sixteen-man Reichstag committee entrusted itself with special consultative rights on any matter of particular interest. The distrust between the soldiers and the civilians again expressed itself and obstructed effective supply methods. "What became of the food dictatorship," snorted the railroad chief. The soldier found it difficult to appreciate the machinery of parliamentary action.

The frustrated Reichstag of World War I did not exactly demonstrate crisis co-operation at its best. Distrust was its heritage and divisive party quarrels its nature. The right and left wings were deeply alien to one another and the bourgeois middle divided unpredictably on every issue. After 1915 the patriotic reconciliation with the government was ended and the sniping attack on the autocratic regime was renewed. The Reichstag moved back into such aggravating problems as Prussian suffrage and gave running discussion to peace plans and war leadership. The conservatives thought the Reichstag might better go home or content itself with enthusiastic support of the war effort. The socialists wanted national economic controls and full suffrage equality. Everybody disagreed on annexations, submarines and peace diplomacy. In short, the Empire was thoroughly at odds with itself by 1916 and hardly co-ordinated for the desperate struggle at hand. Now that spirits were raw and materials scarce, it was a little late for harmonious regulation and contraction.

Groener was one of those who wanted to send the Reichstag home. Let all the parties be represented in a national executive council and let it entrust war leadership to the military. At the same time, the national spirit could be rejuvenated by some significant democratic action, such as suffrage reform. Then a unified and uplifted Germany might be able to thwart Allied pressure and work out a satisfactory peace for itself. According to Groener, the frustrated German people were ready for a military dictatorship in the "firm, naive belief" that the soldiers might still organize success. And a postwar Reichstag investigating committee also judged that the General Staff took charge of Germany mainly because effective civilian leadership was absent. Apparently the coming dictatorship of Ludendorff reflected a national situation as well as a personal arrogation.[9]

The army made its bid for control of the home front in the Fall of 1916. Ludendorff approached Bethmann-Hollweg for a levee en masse in which the High Command would gain authority over every German within a certain age bracket, perhaps between fifteen and sixty. But the Chancellor thought such a request would be quite unacceptable; it would be difficult enough to work a more modest draft of labor through the Reichstag. So the Hindenburg program resorted to a less forward pronunciation of its desiderata. It asked for more soldiers and for more home-front production. Somehow, by a Ludendorff act of will, the German production line was to surrender more men to the army, yet also increase its volume of output. That meant tighter control of raw materials, production and labor. Non-essential work had to stop and a general labor draft was to be invoked. Women and handicapped persons were to be utilized. Organized youth might help out on the farm. The worker was to be forced into war industry and frozen to his job. He must be enlisted in the industrial army and man his station as though he were in uniform.

The entire productive machinery of the Empire was to be given into the hands of the military. Ludendorff understood that his immediate use of more recruits would automatically reduce the reserve strength of the future. That shortage would then have to be counter-balanced by more equipment, machine guns, mortars and cannons. The army's future stability was thus premised on the success of the Hindenburg program. German industry quickly promised Ludendorff astronomical production increase and he counted his immediate reinforcements as a smart loan from the future. [10]

Groener was the choice of the High Command for its planned domestic mobilization, but this time he would have to relinquish his railroad post. He did so reluctantly for here lay his unassailable skill, authority, and happiness. But there was an economic job to be done, so he snapped on the harness and stepped into the Berlin arena. His happy days and unsullied reputation would henceforth move into eclipse. Ahead lay only complex responsibility, insoluble dilemma, harrassing Ludendorff impatience and misunderstood failure.

Before his appointment to the new War Office, he expressed his views about the Hindenburg program to the Chancellor and the dual commanders. He wondered if it might not be better to ask for voluntary response from labor; it might willingly staff an expanding war industry and make a coercive law to that effect unnecessary. He thought the material short-age needed more careful regulation. The idea of female labor was fine but the factories would first have to be made fit for femininity, and he reminded his superiors that the use of un-skilled or handicapped workers would also involve on-the-job training. Having aired some of his views, Groener then pre-pared to assume charge of the new position and escort Luden-dorff's Auxiliary Service Bill ( Hilfsdienstgesetz ) through the Reichstag. His political career was under way. [11]

Groener began to negotiate the bill through Reichstag channels at the end of October, 1916. His co-sponsor was Prussian Minister of the Interior Helfferich. The High Command proposed that every German male between the age of fifteen and fifty-nine be made available to the military authorities for possible assignment to a war job. The War Ministry was to manage such registration and the newly created War Office was to fix industry needs and guide the distribution of man power. Joint local committees, composed of an employer, a labor delegate, and a War Office representative were to select the specific personnel needed. Petition against such committee decisions, or uncertainties about the definition of a war job, were to be decided by the higher echelons of the War Office. Ludendorff wanted to control the mobility of labor within the war industry and all newly constructed German factories were expected to serve War Office needs first. It was recognized that certain industries would be stripped of their labor force and that certain hardships in such a national realignment could not be avoided.

Helfferich, labor, and some of the German states hesitated almost immediately. The Prussian Minister believed in laissez faire and he wondered whether a voluntary labor and

industrial effort could not satisfy requirements. The states
did not welcome such intrusion into their economic affairs.
Whole industries might be laid still and problems of unemploy-
ment created. Labor suspected the motives of the High Command and was hostile to any job freeze. Their lives would
then be even more thoroughly under the control of the military.
Initial discussions of the bill brought questions of detail to
the fore. Where did the division of authority between the War
Office, the War Ministry, and the civilian bureaucracy lay?
How were the rights of labor, or the autonomy of business, to
be regulated and protected? Was it wise to expose such a
controversial measure to the argumentive Reichstag? Some
officials thought it would be wiser to proclaim such action
through the federal Bundesrat. [12]

Groener was irked by such explicit and cautious attention.
He wanted the Auxiliary Service bill to serve as a broad, in-
spiring declaration of intensified effort and national solidarity.
Details could be worked out later. He was willing to include
civilian help and counsel in his War Office, and labor was
promised important representation as well as strong petition
safeguards. Helfferich was prepared to maneuver his way
through the Reichstag but the general looked for quick agreement and deferred questions. He reported such unwelcome
reactions back to Headquarters and asked for another round of
support. So the High Command reassured Groener that its
request must be accepted as it stood. Only then was a "clear
solution" to Germany's dilemma possible. Let the Reichstag
understand that the war could be won "only with the help of
such a law." And it required the "collaboration of the Reichstag, which absolutely must share the burden of responsibility." The High Command wanted Reichstag approval for democratic resonance and appearance but it rejected sincere deliberation. The Reichstag might even assume responsibility in
case things went wrong. [13]

The socialists were not impressed with such imperious
wisdom and they proceeded to work their bridgeheads into the
bill. They were rather pleased with the Head of the new War
Office even though he sponsored a dangerous bill. He spoke
with human directness and evident sincerity. He understood
labor's need and its competitive concern about the conditions
and implications of the Auxiliary Service bill. He guaranteed

fair administration of all industrial matters, high and low.
He even expressed interest in a surplus profits tax as a justifiable corollary to any labor draft. Promises and informal
understandings were broached informally in committee meetings. Groener wanted the bill to come to life and he was
willing to adjust to certain labor modifications. He understood
that German power now rested very substantially on its labor
corps and he realistically accepted their growing place in
German politics. He could admit that the High Command was
not always right, whereas the War Minister insisted a few days
later that the "High Command does not make mistakes." The
same General von Stein who wrote the bulletin had denied defeat at the Marne. Compared to such rigid types, Groener
impressed the Reichstag delegates, and especially the socialists, as a reasonable, intelligent fellow German.

The General Staff and the Social Democrats were emerging
ever more clearly as the two exponents of German force, and
it was Groener's job to correlate the interests of both in the
new domestic mobilization. Success depended on friendly
negotiation and joint national interest on the part of all concerned. His Swabian qualities were suddenly of real value
as the General Staff sought greater civilian sacrifice and help
at home. Groener was at ease in the bourgeois world and he
knew how to talk to the common man. A few words spoken at
a union meeting in December of that year well illustrated his
egalitarian simplicity:

> "I know that we will assist one another in the great-
> est mutual trust. And when the Auxiliary Service
> law is out of force after the war, then we can shake
> one another by the hand and say: we did that with
> real good sense."

He felt, and conveyed, a sincerity and democracy of attitude
which did much to mollify labor's suspicions about the Ludendorff campaign into the home front. [14]

Labor would not allow itself to be completely disarmed by
a personality, least of all in uniform. Groener's impression
notwithstanding, the military request for total mobilization
threatened the freedom of the working citizen and it had to be
modified. In classic parliamentary fashion, a dangerous bill
of four paragraphs was expanded to a porous eighteen. Labor

kept its right to change war jobs and gained important petition
rights and a key representative in the structure of the War Office. And the War Ministry was also given a place in the administration of the new economic effort. That meant stiff old
generals and procedures which would resist the new War Office and alienate the citizens forced into their registry and
processing care. Groener was accustomed to complete authority in his railroad work and now his jurisdiction was to be
carefully regulated, but he stepped into the job with typical
energy with the hope that his considerable arbitration powers
might enable him to shape a system more to his liking.

In his willingness to make concessions to labor, Groener
alienated his own political partner, Helfferich. The latter was
a shrewd and suspicious Minister of the crown who regarded
the Reichstag as the constitutional enemy. The general was
told to get a quick mobilization bill and he did not hesitate
to make concessions as they seemed to be necessary. He was
accustomed to executive independence, but Helfferich was
not always at the Reichstag committee meetings and was not
always kept informed of Groener's spontaneous actions. His
own chary bargaining was thus often undermined by the military partner. He was thoroughly chagrined and annoyed when
the socialist delegates once asked him, "How can you oppose
things which General Groener has long since granted us?"
And probably Helfferich was not too happy when Groener told
him that the war involved the "greatest democratic wave ever
to pass over the nations." One could not oppose such a wave,
one could only "steer with it."[15]

Such democratic determinism on the part of his general
apparently sifted through to the Kaiser. He was in good autocratic form that Fall and impregnable to such thoughts. Even
after the Somme he could still boast to Reichstag delegates,
"where my Guards appear, there is no room for democracy."
There was the equally revealing comment to a conservative
leader,

> "Albert shall keep his Belgium, since he too is King
> by Divine Right.... Though of course he will have
> to toe the line there. I imagine our future relation-
> ship to be rather like that of the Egyptian Khedive
> to the King of England."[16]

When Groener appeared at a royal dinner shortly after the Auxiliary Service law was passed, he felt the cool wind of disfavor. William shook hands with his little finger, a pert sign of displeasure, and later accused his general of being a popularity seeker. The crown simply could not accept a mode of procedure which recognized the Reichstag as a legitimate and dignified organ of the national governing process.

Groener's War Office tackled an impossible assignment. There simply was not enough man power to go around and certain material deficiencies also helped to hamstring productive strength. Ludendorff wanted more men to be released from industry and dispatched to the front lines. At the same time he also wanted higher production quotas. Women, children, and handicapped persons were to staff the reorganized industrial system and give the German army the abundant supply which it hitherto lacked. Ludendorff recognized the difficulty of such a reorganization, with marginal resources everywhere, and yet he apparently thought it could be successfully carried through. But his executive inside Germany soon had very grave doubts.

The labor problem did not involve numbers as much as skill. Germany's skilled man power was in the trenches and now the High Command wanted the rest of it withdrawn from industry. Women and children could not replace their functions. In fact, more women were looking for work than there were positions available, and the few specialists left at home were taking advantage of their Auxiliary Service loophole. They were switching frequently to better paying jobs and the war industry was not on a healthy labor footing. Enterprise contributed its part to the problem by offering higher wages to other workers.

A comparable shortage plagued the matter of raw material distribution and production charting. Industry designed its expansion plans and then applied to the War Office for the necessary supply allocations. Groener's office, in trying to husband its resources and direct an efficient expansion, gave very careful bureaucratic scrutiny to all such industrial requests. There was a discouraging maze of paper-work and War Office inspection. Supply margins were thin and a hitherto untrammeled industrial world suddenly found itself with a military bit in its mouth. They had expected the regimentation of labor, not of production, so they complained privately to Ludendorff that the War Office had created a confusing bureaucratic labyrinth which made it impossible for them to fulfill their production promises.

The winter of 1916-1917 was no help. Industrial expansion meant that the railroads had to haul construction material for the new factories being built. A cold winter froze up the waterways and the railroads assumed even more extra duty. A shortage of lubricating grease caused the entire German transportation system to buckle dangerously. The building program had to stop and all the materials poured into that effort now stood wasted in partly constructed factories and warehouses.

An entire national economy, worn thin by two years of war and blockade, could not simply double or treble production on order of the High Command. Maybe Ludendorff thought the demand for the impossible would bring the possible. Such logic had its limits on the battlefield and it only strained economic stability at home. The forcing haste of the Hindenburg program took hold of the resources left to Germany and wasted a good deal in impetuous expansion. Groener's office could simplify production and bring related industrial processes closer together in order to save on transportation, but it could not create the labor and the raw materials needed, and it was too late for orderly improvisation.

Ludendorff registered his first complaint to Groener late in January, 1917. The munitions stockpile was not building up very rapidly and new factory construction was practically at a standstill. He indicated that there was considerable criticism of the way in which the War Office functioned. In mid-February he elaborated on that comment. The War Office was too ramified; each item of business had to go through many different hands. The subordinates lacked independence of action and had to clear everything through higher channels. There was much uncertainty of procedure and too much redundant deliberation. Certain production matters would get lost for weeks without anyone knowing where the files were. Ludendorff conceded that Groener's system must exercise care and that productive abundance with marginal resources was a difficult undertaking, yet he wondered whether there was not too much paper-work and consultation.

Ludendorff was superficially informed and fundamentally unrealistic in his criticisms. Groener readily admitted that there had been initial confusion and duplication of action. He wanted a careful system and thought proper initial routine more important than a few quick production decisions. He told his people to stress the personal contact with industry and labor; correspondence and memoranda were to be kept on a functional, even first-draft, level. He had never been one to stifle the independence of subordinates and such uncertainty was due only to the novelty of the job itself, but mere system alone could not produce that which Ludendorff needed and which industry had promised. Groener's was a thankless, experimental assignment in which an impulsive Ludendorff, laissez faire habits, and deep labor suspicions were to be dissolved and blended in a magical industrial creation. And all this was to be done with marginal supply, deteriorating railroads, and inadequate labor. Groener could only explain problems to Ludendorff, not solve them, and such wisdom was pointless to the victor of Tannenberg. [17]

Groener's travail continued throughout the severe "turnip winter" and Spring marked Germany's first great munitions strike. Production lagged and worker morale sank to the point of resistance. Far to the east the Russian revolution stirred the hopes and fears of many Germans. Spartacist agitators and Independent Socialist opportunists worked to touch off a mass protest. [18] On the right the German conservatives and super-patriots were just as radical in their stubborn need of victory and continuing autocracy.

A reduction in the bread ration was announced for April 16, and many Germans expected a labor demonstration to take place. Berlin police reports worried about an indifferent and defeatist public. Reichstag delegate Haase asked, on March 30, if the Government wanted the masses to start talking "Russian." The war censorship office cautioned the newspapers not to deal carelessly with the Russian revolution, for fear of irritating class antagonisms and further weakening the German stand. A strike "lay in the air" and the authorities in Berlin got ready for it. Groener urged that labor be given timely representation on the food agencies. The Prussian Ministry of the Interior asked the police to be cautious and refrain from calling in the military unless a crisis actually did arise, the army must not be used against the public. And the Majority socialists were afraid that mass disturbances might lead to a complete militarization of the economy or to an uncontrollable, revolutionary rip-tide.

About 200,000 workers walked out of the Berlin armament factories on the morning of April 16. Some of the strikers marched toward government office areas and others went out to the parks for a day of relaxation. A few bakeries were looted but public order generally prevailed. The police had discreetly broken up the drift toward the government office areas and there was no mass procession. Groener's War Office and the Prussian Government promised the workers more food and direct representation in the food distribution agencies, but this quiet emotional release and protest could not be dispelled in a day or two.

Some workers returned to their jobs on April 17, but such pacification was more than counterbalanced by the appearance of a political petition from Leipzig demanding peace without annexation, equal suffrage, nullification of the Auxiliary Service law, the termination of martial law and the censorship of the press. It also asked that the Chancellor receive a delegation of strikers from Leipzig. The demonstration moved into political gear and the action of the government was critically important. Majority socialists Ebert and Scheidemann urged the workers to reject such explosive political demands, and the union leaders barely managed to swing their groups against the Leipzig resolution. The same union leaders asked their men to return to work on April 18, and the organized nerve of the strike was broken. A Hindenburg appeal for home front loyalty appeared in the newspapers on April 20, and Groener asked labor for "unstinting co-operation" with the War Office. Most of the strikers went back to work although new trouble loomed ahead for the traditional socialist May Day.

On April 21, Groener met in a general council with other military and Prussian government leaders. They agreed that a military fight with labor must be avoided to the last and that an effort should be made to pick off the leaders instead. The central meeting of the metal unions on April 22 would soon show labor's further course of action. That meeting was postponed and Groener knew that the union leaders had regained control and would not further challenge the government.

Now with the trend moving back toward law and order a-gain, Groener employed a more decisive tone. His report to the Main Committee of the Reichstag discussed the strike as an understandable psychological outburst. The Leipzig demands and the propaganda material uncovered first gave the strike its dangerous aspect. Groener warned that there were to "be no more strikes" and that he would "proceed ruthlessly" against any instigators. At the same time, he reassured labor that he would defend their rights under the Auxiliary Service law. He and the War Office were "absolutely neutral."[19]

On the following day, April 27, Groener addressed himself to the broad German public. He referred to Hindenburg's call for unity and arms.

> "Who dares defy Marshal von Hindenburg's call? He is a scoundrel who strikes while our armies face the enemy... Our worst enemies are in the midst of us. They are the faint-hearted,...the strike agitators.... He is a coward who listens to their words. Read what the Imperial Penal Code says about high treason. Who dares to refuse work when Marshal von Hindenburg demands it?... We are not far from the goal. The existence of our people is at stake."

Hindenburg's letter and Groener's "manifesto" were to be posted on all factory bulletin boards where labor might be properly reprimanded and inspired. The tone was patriotic and strident, obviously colored by the revolutionary experience of the moment. Groener's own views were not that simple or optimistic.

Not only did Groener address himself to the Reichstag and to the public; he also resorted to private influence. He literally cornered Independent Socialist leader Haase in the Reichstag committee room to tell him that any May Day demonstration would be met with gunfire. Haase was too cautious for that sort of a climax and he assured Groener "that under no circumstances would there be a strike" on that day. All in all, the authorities had scouted and controlled the strike with flexible skill. It lacked real leadership and a crisis situation, but it could well have developed into a turbulent, explosive street battle. Groener's anti-revolutionary experience was

now begun, even as he realized that the Hohenzollern government must ride with the reform wave or else capsize. [20]

Groener received no thanks for his defense of the state in
that April moment of danger. The conservatives could not understand his initial laxity toward the strike and the socialists
were offended by his crude denunciation and naive appeal.
"One does not speak to free, thinking workers like that," said
socialist Bauer in the Reichstag. "The workers do not take
orders from the military. They laugh at such language and are
not at all impressed." And Groener assured his socialist
critics that he had phrased the "Hundsfott" charge with care
and he out-flanked them by exhibiting a collection of revolutionary leaflets which clearly showed that the strike was more
than a mere cry of hunger. His unfortunate battle with labor
was then terminated with a letter from the Trade Unions which
upheld the logic of Groener and Hindenburg, "Strikes at the
present time must be avoided; the preservation and security
of the Empire take first place." [21]

That letter of reassurance from the Trade Unions expressed
labor's complaint, as well as its loyalty. Black market luxu-
ries were still easily available to the rich. The Auxiliary
Service law mobilized labor and often countenanced personal
hardship, but it did not require better working conditions or
raise pay levels. Groener understood the basic discrimination
and dissatisfaction. The law chafed the working man more
than it did the industrialist. The latter could dodge paper regulations, pile up excessive war profits, and find emergency
help from Ludendorff when necessary.

The April strike convinced Groener that the German situation was grim and in need of early peace. Such home-front
instability further doomed the Hindenburg program and the
foundations of German strength. The Russian revolution promised to neutralize a front, but it also heightened the danger of
a social explosion within the Hohenzollern empire. Now was
the time to negotiate a settlement in the west and renew the
loyalty of the German people with democratic reforms. Groener
tried to convey his thoughts to the Kaiser. He had a longer
talk with the Empress telling her about the blockade and the
hardship which it brought to the common people. She was
sympathetic and eager to help, but she still thought only in
terms of charity and seemingly did not comprehend that gracious

concern was no longer enough. The people wanted rights and care. Apparently the Empress did help Groener get another invitation to a royal dinner where he tried to get the Kaiser's ear, but to no avail. The latter sparkled with entertaining chit-chat and almost seemed intent on avoiding any serious exchange with his controversial general.

Having failed at the palace, Groener then expressed himself to Chancellor Bethmann-Hollweg and to Valentini, head of the Kaiser's personal cabinet. He reminded them that victory might not be possible and that it was time to prepare the nation for something less. The step from "non-victory to defeat was not very big" but the shock to an unprepared public could have revolutionary ramifications. Let the events in Russia serve as a timely warning. He expressed similar thoughts to other conservative leaders, among then Ludendorff's friend Hugo Stinnes. They all agreed that the German situation was precarious, but they could not accept the suffrage reform and the socialistic monarchy which Groener thought necessary to the day. Stinnes insisted stoutly that "Ludendorff will win." To which Groener flatly retorted, "Ludendorff will not win."

Groener finally received a visitor himself in the person of the Kaiser's military adjutant, General von Plessen. In the halcyon days of August, 1914, this old friend of Schlieffen repeatedly led Groener into the Kaiser's presence. Then victory seemed near and the railroad chief stood as an admired disciple of the Schlieffen school, but now Plessen had other thoughts on his heart. He charged that Groener seemed intent on warning the Kaiser that this was impossible. Groener should give up any further attempt to see His Majesty. Groener indicated that realistic frankness was also an obligation of duty but he agreed to the Plessen demand. Let the Kaiser's friends be responsible for the Hohenzollern future.

The word was passed around that General Groener was "letting his tail hang; it might be good to send him to the front." That might straighten out his logic and revitalize his will. Berlin was full of faltering patriots that Summer and Groener was not alone in his search for an early peace. A Reichstag majority supported the July Peace Resolution of Matthias Erzberger. It evasively spoke "for a peace of understanding" and did not categorically renounce the possibility of territorial acquisitions. It had a tone of adroit, rather than sincere, good will, but it did express a German recognition that the war could not be won and must be terminated. As Friedrich Naumann wrote, it was "decision time in German history." Only the men of realistic national interest lost out to the Prussian junkers and the industrial tycoons. These men controlled the Kaiser and the army, and they were not interested in a compromise peace. They could even baldly admit that they would rather bring Germany to ruin than accept a compromise peace and consequent democratic reform at home. Bethmann-Hollweg was forced to resign and his effort to find some "diagonal" link between autocracy and democracy, victory and peace, was cast aside. [22]

As the High Command maneuvered its way through the peace crisis that summer, Groener threw his own bomb into the Ludendorff ranks. He submitted a memorandum to the government which recommended stringent national control of both wages and profits. He had favored such action from the very beginning of his War Office assignment and, in the negotiations over the Auxiliary Service bill, he even prompted the socialist delegates to promote the idea in the Reichstag. An aide by the name of Merton wrote the memorandum and Groener had it personally delivered to Chancellor Michaelis as he assumed office in late July. It would disappear into the files and, in the Spring of 1918, have its very existence denied by the government on the Reichstag floor. Even then, the original draft lay in the files of the War Office. The memorandum which Groener submitted finally turned up after the war, with marginal comments by Helfferich who happened to be the chief protagonist of a laissez faire economy. [23]

The memorandum accused the German entrepeneur of attuning his war business methods to the profit lure and not to the patriotic need. He insisted on the maintenance of free enterprise, but he did not hesitate to gouge the state on war contracts. The wages of labor were often far too low and it quickly emulated enterprise in demanding what the market might pay. Since industry could always match pay raises with higher prices, a price spiral was begun which was both costly and disastrous to the nation's fiscal stability. Germans liked to sneer at English merchant zeal but that country had been quick to regulate its economic life in support of the war effort.

The memorandum urged that wages be fixed, every contract cost set at the beginning of production, and all profit taxed to the hilt. The government should be given the right to seize any industry and operate it in accordance with the law. "Enterprise must clearly understand that war is no time for money making but that it requires actual sacrifice, involuntary if necessary, from everyone." Such discipline now would also prepare the German economy for the difficult postwar adjustments.

A few weeks later, Groener was removed from the War Office and assigned to a division on the western front. He recognized his isolation and indicated his readiness to go, should Ludendorff think a change opportune. The Hindenburg program was not fulfilled and the Auxiliary Service law remained rather ineffective. A certain mobilization of labor and simplification of production took place, but prices, wages, and profits spiralled steadily upwards as workers and enterprise alike pulled clear of regulation. Groener's office and person attracted a lengthening line of critics and his transfer seemed to be due.

The manner of his release was more objectionable than objective. He made a routine visit to Ludendorff on August 15 and discussed various business matters with him. There was no indication of a possible change. On returning to Berlin the following morning, Groener read in the newspaper that he was being transferred. The official orders followed later that day. Groener suspected that big industry had learned of the Merton memorandum and pushed for his removal. A week before his removal, industrialist Duisberg was reported to have informed a group of his associates that Groener "was through." The suspicions of Groener were probably valid but there were also other reasons why his transfer seemed desirable. [24]

The conservative newspapers shrugged off his removal as just another administrative move. The socialists saluted him as a man who respected the equality of labor in the German social complex. This general had more regard for their problems than did the civilian government. The Frankfurter Zeitung described him as a man who actually did not "know any parties" and truly sought to serve the national interest. The picture of this energetic and friendly general, chatting casually with the socialists at their own caucus table in the Reichstag, represented the kind of civility and social harmony which that great newspaper espoused for modern Germany. [25]

Groener was not able to subordinate both labor and industry to centralized military control. Full authority was not granted by the suspicious civilians and the different German parts continued to move independently within the Empire system. Labor sensed its growing strength in the Reichstag and on the Berlin streets. Industry found access to the tent of Ludendorff. The compromise bourgeois parties in the middle floated helplessly between these two poles of power. Groener tried to reconcile labor and the army but he was successful only in a personal fashion. Suspicion of the High Command remained and his War Office could not muster a _levee en masse_ at a time when resources and spirit were already beyond rally by command. Groener recognized that German strength and stability were at the breaking point and he spoke up for domestic and diplomatic adjustments which made him an appeaser. The general was sent to the troops where he could watch his fears come true.

Chapter Five

## THE LIQUIDATION RESPONSIBILITY

Groener's division was on a quiet sector of the Lorraine front where he had a chance to refresh his spirit and reflect on the German problem. It was too late for exaggerated patriotism or military heroics, and the zeal of Ludendorff and his faction no longer served the national interest. They could not win and they would not make peace. Let Ludendorff try to make the kind of a peace "which the All-Germans regale him with." Such naive and selfish militancy could only bring the weakening nation to a point of complete helplessness and social collapse. The wage-price spiral would wipe out the middle class and add another wing to the dissatisfied proletariat. The vigorous socialists would rebel rather than dutifully serve the High Command.

Two naive soldiers were left in charge of German destiny at a time when caution and slyness were imperative. Groener felt sure that this old guard could not successfully harness the new German currents coming to the surface. It was now clear that the modern state could find stability only if it satisfied the working class and cultivated the good will of the public. Let the people "feel themselves" to be governed in a liberal fashion. That ideological vogue must somehow be satisfied, even if only in a superficial way.[1]

His own troops certainly were in no mood for romantic heroics. Theirs had become an animalistic fight for life and they were dull to any problem or promise except the dream of peace. Tales and pep talks were no longer welcome. Groener kept All-German patriotic leaflets away from his men because he thought they would cause more anger than enthusiasm. Groener wondered whether they had the sufficiency of strength and equipment to sustain a final victory offensive. But it was still a hardened, muscular force which knew how to fight and die. With them, Ludendorff and Germany would make one more climatic effort to force a victory in the west.

Again Groener preferred operations elsewhere. As he wrote to his wife in early January, 1918, "Ten Hindenburgs and Ludendorffs cannot effect the superiority of men, weapons and munitions really necessary to finish a fight in the west." Offensive action against the less formidable armies in Italy and the Balkans impressed him as being the more astute German strategy. The Russian revolution crumbled the eastern front, and now Germany could buttress such new hinterland security and expansion with victories along the Mediterranean. Then the Empire might yet wedge out a profitable peace for itself.

Now and then Groener could still dream of a happy end, for his Staatsraeson responded to the opportunities, as well as the necessities, of power. But he also recognized that the German public expected a major victory effort in the west. Ludendorff told him it had to be ventured. Home-front morale was weakening, as were allies Turkey and Austria-Hungary. The American troops would soon be pouring into France to make that front even more impregnable. It would be a colossal struggle, but an immediate strike for victory in the west should not be deferred. [2]

Groener dubiously hoped for the best and watched the German army settle into its starting blocks, but he was destined to watch, rather than share, in that final failure of the General Staff. In early February he was transferred to the Ukrainian theatre where he was to organize food shipments to Germany and keep the new Ukrainian government clear of Bolshevik control. Ludendorff wanted economic help for Germany, and Berlin wanted a ring of satellite states to be formed around Bolshevik Russia. So Groener made the long train ride to Brest-Litowsk and on to Kiev. He was chief of staff in a corps which controlled an area more than twice as large as Germany, but again his assignment could only partially be fulfilled.

The Ukrainian grain bin was empty. Years of war had strained agricultural production; months of revolution disrupted it. German soldiers moved into a land where orderly economic life had ceased. What the peasants needed for themselves, they hid in underground caches. Neither the Germans nor the Bolsehviks could locate these, and for Groener's purposes they were insignificant. He soon realized that Ukraine was not going to satisfy the German supply expectations. As he told his wife: Berlin thinks that Ukraine is a well stocked larder and that I am the magician who can send grain and hogs to the homeland. "How to get this on a freight train, or if there even is one, does not give those people much of a headache."

Groener was not very happy with the young idealists who were trying to establish the Ukrainian People's Republic. They talked of dividing the large estates and neither their plans nor their actions were very helpful to German supply interests. The government in Berlin recognized this Ukrainian regime because it was anti-Bolshevik, but Groener saw little economic profit in their experiments and he leaned toward the large landholders and immediate stability. His job was to set up a supply base and he was not interested in diplomatic logic or ideological sentimentalities. He complained to Ludendorff and Berlin that the incumbent Ukrainian government could not ensure the needed grain deliveries and he asked for stronger German leadership.

Apparently his clearance came through. On April 23 he consulted with emissaries from the German and Austro-Hungarian foreign offices. On the following day he discussed the situation with General Skoropadski, a Ukrainian nobleman and spokesman for the large landholders. On April 28 a detachment of German troops broke into the Ukrainian Assembly (Rada), dispersed the delegates and arrested some of the government ministers. Groener said their action was unauthorized and his superior, General Eichorn, expressed his regrets. But both German leaders were quick and happy to deal with the new government of General Skoropadski. His aversion for socialistic experiments complemented their own and he promised to give them the foodstuffs they were looking for. The Skiropadski regime dissolved the Rada, placed the Ukrainian army under German control and agreed to reimburse the Germans for their military help. It also restored large estates to their landlords and agreed to a forthcoming military and economic pact with Germany. Such were German satellite policies in a beginning drive to exploit eastern weakness.

Groener chortled happily over his <u>coup</u>.

> "People on the street say that the German command
> has conducted this overthrow and they are not very
> far from wrong. It just would not go with the old
> regime any more and a strong cuff across the ear,
> which they earned, was enough to unseat such
> youngsters from their ministerial stools."

Public order was much improved under Skoropadski but produce shipments did not increase. The Ukrainians could not
deliver their promised quotas of fruits, fats, eggs, and live-
stock. The Germans also fell short on their deliveries of coal,
agricultural machinery, and other manufactured products. Both
societies were exhausted by war and all the exhortation by
Groener and Skoropadski was futile. Just as Ludendorff could
not command industrial sufficiency in Germany, so now did
Groener pull fruitlessly at an exhausted, disinterested
Ukrainian people. There were not enough German soldiers and
Skoropadskis to muster the land. There was not even enough
seed in the ground, or peasants at the hoe.

In Ukraine, Groener got a firsthand look at revolutionary
disorder and collapse. "God protect us," he wrote to his wife
about the initial socialist leaders, "from such chaos and a
government which has possibly the finest ideas for human
happiness but cannot act for all its ideas and talk." That
grim impression of a disintegrated society would serve to guide
Groener's values and decisions in the German trial to come.[3]

Under Skoropadski, life in Kiev settled into an occupation
routine for Groener and he could direct his main worry to the
west, where the Ludendorff offensive gambled for victory or
defeat. The first drive toward Amiens almost broke through,
but Foch plugged the hole and succeeded in shouldering the
German advance away from the coast. Much ground was gained
by the Germans but the Allied line still stood intact. Groener
wanted Amiens and its transportation facilities. "When Amiens
is taken and the British right flank north of the Somme is
wedged away from the river—then we can shoot the victory
salute and hang out the flags." But that fleeting dream soon
passed on as the second drive for the Channel ports was well
contained. Ludendorff's victory offensive was finished and
he should have contracted for defense again. His bulging ad-
vances merely represented lengthier front-line commitments

for a tiring army. He, the Crown Prince, and many others recognized as early as June that Germany's ability to assert itself militarily was now in terminal decline. Ludendorff even consulted with Foreign Secretary Kuehlmann about preparations for a negotiated peace. Kuehlmann's ventilation of that fact in the Reichstag stung the pride of the High Command and he was disavowed and forced out of office. [4]

A third German drive was then instantaneously crushed at Chateau-Thierry and three days later the Allied counteroffensive began with a startling penetration at Villers-Cotterets. The German retreat began and when a Guards division panicked on August 8, it symbolized the beginning of the end. Both Ludendorff and the Kaiser agreed at a crown council on August 14 that the war must be ended, but they decided to wait for a more propitious tactical moment before making their truce interests public. The High Command simply could not face up to the fact that the war was irretrievably lost and that diplomatic negotiations could not forever be postponed. As they waited, their army's collapse became ever more evident and the German diplomats would have less to bargain with in the weeks and months to come.

Groener watched helplessly from Kiev as the German army began to stumble and reel. He encouraged his wife to take things in disciplined stride but his own spirit had to work its way through the agony of defeat. He waited hopelessly for his army to hold off the Allied attacks after July 18. He waited for the Ukrainian harvest which might give new life to the hungry peoples of the Central Powers, but it was a damp, rainy summer. Three days after the demoralizing defeat of August 8, he too finally gave up the ghost. He wrote from the eastern hinterland,

> "A dreary and cold rainy day hangs over Kiev and depresses my spirit. What is going to happen to the harvest with weather like we have been having? Is it raining right in the middle of the harvest at home too? Good God, have you become an American, or what is going on? At the moment things look very serious in the west. Despite the U-boats, more Americans have come over than we anticipated."

Ludendorff had chanced too much and now the consequences

were unavoidable. As a delegate of the Center party had confidently predicted a few months back, "the sword brought us peace in the east, it will also bring us peace in the west." That was the Ludendorff gamble and it became the German destiny.[5]

The Allies now had the Germans tired and off balance, and they struck vigorously to harvest their advantage. Foch concentrated on collapsing the several German salients which protruded into his line. A highly successful American attack at St. Mihiel then dangerously loosened the southern anchor of the German armies in Belgium and northern France. A penetration here could slice right up the Meuse and break up the German right flank. Foch now decided to launch a general offensive pivoting on Verdun and rolling up the Antwerp-Meuse line. If he could interdict the German rail line running from Metz through Sedan to the north, then the logistical agility of the entire enemy front would be seriously impaired. The American army at Verdun was closest to this line and its progress would be a critical barometer of strategic developments.

In late September, Groener made a visit to Berlin and the western front. The Headquarters people at Spa told him that the situation was critical but Hindenburg and Ludendorff were quietly poised. Groener asked Ludendorff for the truth. "The situation is serious," answered the latter, "but in no way immediately threatening." In fact the Allied armies were in the process of re-grouping. Groener asked how long the army could hold out. "We must have peace by Christmas," was the answer. The entire impression at Headquarters was one of disciplined resignation.

A few days later Ludendorff's request for an immediate armistice was conveyed to a select Reichstag group. Strangely enough, the Reichstag was again included in his unpleasant commission of responsibility. Now they could be involved in government as representatives of the people and counsel to a losing peace. Ludendorff's emissary reported that the Allied offensive had resumed and the Bulgarian defection signalled the break-up of the Balkan front. "Every twenty four hours," he said, "can impair the situation and give our opponent the opportunity of clearly realizing" the German predicament. Groener's Berlin friends were greatly distressed but he took the news with a grain of salt. Inured to Ludendorff's impatience, he regarded this report as merely a technique to hurry the German diplomats into action. Actually they had been held back by the High Command itself as it chose to wait for more favorable news from the front. Now Ludendorff wanted a truce immediately to preserve whatever strength and territory there was left to his army. [6]

Hans Delbrueck judged this armistice demand of the High Command to be one of the great diplomatic blunders of the war. Fittingly enough, it was another military decision. It announced to the enemy and to the German people that the Imperial army was finished. How could the German diplomats bargain with such an open confession of weakness? The Allies could now wait for the Germans to crack completely. And on the home front, Ludendorff's action formally opened the revolutionary season. "Now we have them," cried Haase to his fellow Independent Socialist Ledebour. Now they could agitate against a defeated government and plot their revolutionary strategy in step with the exposures and angry shock sure to come. [7]

Ludendorff's confession of weakness did reach Allied ears and it disarmed Germany's subsequent negotiation with Wilson. The idealist shrewdly exploited his strength and unfolded terms in step with mounting military success. Groener was not surprised and beyond shock. Allied dominance allowed the American arbiter mundi to impose rather than negotiate. Three letters in those last days at Kiev well reflected Groener's mood and thought on the eve of German defeat:

(October 18). "Many sad and depressing thoughts pass through my mind these days; I cannot write them even to you. I must first digest innerly that which oppresses me in this most difficult hour of the German people, since I see no way out and I have feared this for several years because we were stricken with blindness.... Ludendorff chanced the last throw and lost. It was beyond our strength!.... There is no point in delivering funeral orations about the past if we would only finally learn to look truth soberly in the eye. I fear, however, that many of our people are still far from recognizing the truth and Great Headquarters, which should have

considered its responsibility to honor tne truth, shies
from it because it fears the loss of trust and confidence in the army. . . . Our strength is fading, militarily and economically, whereas that of our enemy
is still in the ascendant. God grant our government
and Great Headquarters united wisdom and strength."

(October 23). "The present government cannot be
held accountable for that which now follows naturally out of the past self-deception of our high military leaders. It is true that this government lost its
head as Hindenburg opened its eyes to our military
situation. The disappointment was simply too great
after having heard for years of victory, and Hindenburg and Ludendorff were celebrated as victors this
last Spring for their unfortunate offensive.  Such
mistakes take their toll in the life of nations as well
as of individuals.  Our entire people slipped into
self-deception through the shining material ascent
of the last decades, and they became fixed in the
thought that our strength was invincible. We plunged
into world politics before we secured our continental
position and without adequate military preparation."

(October 25). "The will of a merciless tragedy has
struck the German people. The man whom fate gave
to the Kaiser as his related spirit, to whom the ruler
bowed completely—Ludendorff—the hope of all Old-
Prussian and All-German circles, must now become
the grave-digger of the Prussian monarchy. For I
still hope that the German monarchy might be saved
in the fall of the Prussian. Prussia must be dissolved
in the Reich. The obstructions are yet too great and
it is not yet clear whether the present government
can even keep the monarchy alive and healthy.  It
is a pity that we missed the psychological moments
for certain political developments during the war.
Always we come too late with our decisions, which
are then wrestled through in difficult moments, at
the cost of the government."[8]

Groener did not know then that the last scene of this

tragedy was reserved for him.  Ludendorff was unwilling to stay at the death-bed of the Old Prussian monarchy and Groener was called to its side instead.  He became one of that group which was not "accountable" for defeat, but which had to minister to Germany's distress and burdens.  He was the unhappy soldier who looked "truth soberly in the eye" and finally blurted out its fatal meaning for the disbelieving Hohenzollern.  And he was thereafter villified as the general who abandoned the Kaiser, whereas Prussian heroes Ludendorff and Hindenburg were memorialized in the junker hall of fame.

Ludendorff made his exit in late October, but only after asking for a last-ditch levee en masse against the advancing Allies.  His interest in a truce disappeared once he realized that the Allies would require the complete withdrawal and neutralization of the German army.  He was even willing to enlist Social Democrat Ebert as an inspirational leader for such a national resistance effort,  but that party was much more interested in seeing the Kaiser and his paladins go.

Ludendorff's convulsive logic made an especially poor impression on the new government as he briefed a crown council on October 17.  He forecast that the next four weeks would be critical.  He sensed that the Allied attacks were coming to an end,  but he also expected another in the Verdun area on the following day.  Without Rumanian oil Germany could fight only for six more weeks.  He could not promise that his army's position would be improved in four weeks.  War was a matter of luck.  If he could have more men he could face the future with confidence again.  The situation could become critical only if the army suffered defeat near Verdun, otherwise the immediate danger was slight.  The new Chancellor, Prince Max of Baden,  was amazed by such a garbled analysis from this man who was generally recognized as a military genius. Eight days later the High Command tried to force the government into breaking off the negotiations with the United States. For once the Kaiser stood by his Chancellor and accepted Ludendorff's resignation. [9]

The civil government recovered authority in Germany just in time to direct the surrender.  A relieved Kaiser and the steadfast Hindenburg sifted for a new executive commander and they settled on Groener.  Other officers of stature were either unavailable or unwilling.  Groener's matchless transportation

skill would be invaluable in the pending withdrawal and demobilization. Prince Max esteemed his political comprehension
and the Majority Socialists whose good will and co-operation
were critically necessary if the monarchy was to be kept alive
appreciated him as a fair-minded practitioner of the national
interest. Those who still hoped to fight clear of surrender
were dismayed by the appointment. As the Crown Prince said,
he "possessed none of that spirit which alone could save what
was to be saved." His salvage values were of course far different from those of Groener. [10]

Groener received his call in Kiev on October 26. He was
being brought in to liquidate Germany's military enterprise and
he knew that it would be a thankless assignment. As he told
his colleagues on leaving, "I understand very clearly that I
will have to play the goat. There is no longer any honor to be
gained from this appointment." But he went in duty and responsibility, perhaps even with a grain of gallows-pride. He
was at the side of Hindenburg, and the much criticized "southern German democrat" was being asked to help rescue crown
and army. Like the new government, he feared revolution the
most and his experience in Ukraine decisively colored his reaction to the problems and alternatives ahead. A unified nation and its army must be kept intact at all cost, in bourgeois
form and under monarchic direction if possible. He was proud
of the General Staff and convinced of its vital importance to
national stability and recovery. For even as Groener prepared
to accept the humilities and problems of defeat, he nurtured
**the** will to stubborn national survival and recovery.

Sinking Germany was in a fever of crisis change and danger. By late October the press openly discussed the justice
and advantage of abdication. The public expected a sacrifice
and many believed the Kaiser's departure meant better truce
terms. The socialist newspaper, Vorwaerts, reminded one and
all that the shipwreck of the state had "certain consequences...
for the captain." Which leader would explain the situation
and its requirement to the Kaiser? Time was all-important.
Radicals plotted to ride the tidal wave of public disillusionment to power and, as October ended, most of Germany's newspapers and public figures regarded abdication as a necessary
and effective palliative of revolutionary anger. The bourgeois
leaders and the Majority Socialists needed a symbol of decisive

reform if they were to keep a bridle on public feeling. A letter
by Walther Rathenau illustrated this acute fear of Bolshevik
disintegration,

> "Momentarily the danger of Bolshevism is the great-
> est threat. Its containment is more important than
> any other state problem. If this movement ever
> breaks loose, military or administrative containment
> will be impossible."

His fear was representative and absolutely basic to the tactics and considerations of Prince Max and Groener. Most
Germans wanted reform but not radical revolution. Their nation had not been unhappy like Old Russia, nor did it want to
be revolutionary like New Russia. [11]

On October 31 Austria-Hungary informed Berlin of its decision to sue for peace. It signified the collapse of the eastern and southern front, and magnified the necessity of immediate German surrender. The anti-Imperial mood began to
crest as preserving reformers and destructive revolutionaries
raced for leadership of the public. The government of Prince
Max recognized the climactic moment of crisis and decided to
ask the Kaiser for abdication. Such voluntary action might
cushion both liberal and conservative feeling and make a suc-
cession within the dynasty possible. The Kaiser anticipating
the request fled fermenting Berlin for the security of the military headquarters at Spa. There he explained that the government desired his abdication and that he could better oppose
such action from the midst of his army. He told the astounded
Berlin officials that he had to install General Groener in his
new post and that war frequently necessitated such spontaneous moves. In effect he left government and nation to
solve their own problems.

Groener passed through Berlin en route to Spa and he
registered the rebellious restlessness of the home front.
Desperately hoping for the loyal solidarity of army and nation,
he feared that the removal of the Kaiser would demoralize the
officer class and trigger a flight to federalism. Already the
officers were being upset by rumors that William and Hindenburg were in exit, and it was public knowledge that Bavaria
was leaning toward secession. On October 31 an entire division balked and one of Groener's first reports to Berlin

described weakening morale and discipline. He believed the Kaiser question was undermining the army's spirit and in a letter to Payer he asked for the restriction of further abdication polemic. Groener warned that the monarchic officers would honor their oath of loyalty to William and would not accept an artifically installed regent. But the Berlin government persisted in its effort for abdication and Prussian Minister of the Interior Drews courageously undertook to present the abdication problem in the Spa lair itself. The Kaiser received him in the company of Generals Plessen, Hindenburg, and Groener.

Drews relayed the Berlin analysis. Abdication might induce better truce terms. If these were unacceptable, a final levee en masse was hardly possible without a crown change. The government desired voluntary action in order to neutralize further weakening dissension over the matter. William wondered how a sworn Prussian official could participate in such a mission. He and Hindenburg warned of leaderless anarchy in the army and at home. William affirmed that he had also sworn an oath to Germany and he was not going to break his bond. The royal princes had already expressed their refusal to continue the dynasty at the father's expense. He would lead his troops back and restore order. Then Groener chimed in to charge the government with grave neglect in its tolerance of anti-Imperial propaganda which was infecting and debilitating the front-line morale. National survival depended on loyal solidarity. Such words heartened the Kaiser who said to his official, "Now a Wuerttemberger has been forced to tell you what is proper for a Prussian patriot." Drews was somewhat deaf and the angry men in uniform made sure he heard. He too flared up in defense of his position and for a moment a verbal storm resounded in the villa. When the Kaiser recovered he quietly told the distraught emissary to return and "give my opinion to the gentlemen in Berlin." The government's first formal request for abdication had been rejected.

William was pleasantly surprised by the erstwhile "southern German democrat." He told his adjutant,

"You should have seen how the Field Marshal placed himself in front of his Kaiser! —and that the quiet Groener could become so aroused. He told Drews

where the main danger to the fatherland lies: not
in the superior power of our enemies but in the dis-
cord and rebelliousness at home. How gratifying
that it was a south German general who stepped
into the breach for the German Kaiser and the Prussian King."

The Kaiser was still sure of his army and again confident of
Imperial authority. His steady nerve in those days of disintegration showed both crisis courage and blindness. [12]
     The south German general quickly regretted his sharp
treatment of Drews. In subsequent quiet he realized the in-
nocence of the messenger and the significance of his message.
Political leaders whom he respected had concluded that timely
and voluntary abdication promised a better peace and preven-
tion of revolution. Berlin's Foreign Office emissary at Spa
continued the pressure by asking Groener to speak to Hindenburg about a death-seeking front line appearance for the
Kaiser. A day after the Drews scene, Groener did remark to
Hindenburg, Marshall, and Plessen that the Kaiser's position had become "untenable." "Honorable" death or injury at
the front might best save the monarchy and possibly even
arouse the nation to heroic resistance. Plessen, one of the
arch-protagonists of a fight to the finish, refused to take him
seriously. And Hindenburg's comment was equally unheroic,
"then we would no longer have a Kaiser." [13] These Hohenzollern vassals still respected His Majesty's person and will
above all else, but more Germans, like Groener, were beginning to worry that they might no longer have a nation.
     Groener's inspection of the front confirmed his sense of
finality. The straining line was thin in depth and man power.
Rear depots bulged with soldiers who heeded neither command
nor plea to fight. Discipline was often a bargain among
equals and many exchanged combat promises for immediate
furloughs. More were up front in their hopeless stand, waiting for a responsible government to relieve them. A last
desperation offensive project bore the appropriate code name,
Hagen. As Groener remembered, "there was really nothing
left." Even Ludendorff admitted on October 17 that the fighting man was at the limit of his nerve and strength. One friend
wrote to Groener, "Yet have we fulfilled our duty. Every day

gives witness of that. But the moment of collapse moves dangerously near." And the strategic situation was growing
equally desperate.

In Kiev, Groener wondered why the extended right flank
was not disengaged earlier and entrenched in a line running
from Antwerp south along the Meuse to Verdun, but Ludendorff
and Hindenburg wanted all of Belgium for bargaining power at
the truce table. Their fighting withdrawal against superior
strength cost heavily and eventually grappled their exhausted
armies to the Allied bear-hug. Workers began to scrape out
an Antwerp-Meuse-Verdun fortification line in October but it
was a belated move. The American drive toward Sedan threatened the supply system and the logistical mobility of the entire right flank. This was the "dangerous point" which Ludendorff stressed in his last report to the government and its
implications haunted Groener as well. He ordered his right
flank to withdraw to the Meuse-Antwerp line but American
progress was already loosening the southern anchor of that
projected new front, and the German army in defense of this
key pivot area was badly extended and caught west of the
Meuse. The imminent fall of Sedan would prevent the rescue
of its men and material knocking out the base of the right flank
and disjointing the entire German line.

On his inspection trip Groener spoke with the commanders
of that imperiled Fifth army at Sedan. He reassured the Crown
Prince and his executive officer, Schulenburg, that the German army and ruler were still in firm unity. Obviously he con-
tradicted his own already expressed opinion that the Kaiser's
position had become "untenable." He did not suggest to the
son that the father should seek an "honorable" end at the front.
As a Wuerttemberg officer, Groener was inclined to seek convenient and natural neutrality on the crown question, but as
a Wuerttemberg nationalist he was also resolved not to allow
the sacrifice of the German state for the Prussian dynasty.
Torn between responsibility and duty, he fluctuated between
discreet suggestion and loyal resolve. It was an ambiguous
stand but the choice of nation or commander was not easy and
to be delayed as long as possible.

On November 4 Groener left for Berlin in response to a
call from Prince Max. Not only did the Chancellor desire a
military report but he also hoped that the visit might better

focus Groener's comprehension of the home front problem. Groener's Berlin friends expected him to serve as a medium for conducting realistic government desiderata into the inner command circle, and they were apparently surprised by his part in the Drews mission.[14] But his effort to convey the "suicide" idea into the royal circle promised a more favorable receptivity to the needs of Berlin. Groener took the long night ride to the capital city and undoubtedly there were hours of gloomy reflection, punctured by spasms of angry regret. The punishment for the disregard of Schlieffen was at hand. Ruler and people had carelessly dissipated their strength and now they had to "drink the bitter cup to the dregs." He had warned earlier than most and been disgraced for it. How should he choose if the alternative between revolution or abdication actually was unavoidable?

Groener's report to the government on November 5 drew a somber picture of encirclement, weariness and Bolshevik danger. The Allies were pressing toward Germany's western frontier and he could only withdraw if he was to save the army from a "decisive defeat." Germany might still maintain its occupation force in Ukraine and thus hold off the Bolshevik threat in the east, but if the nation and the army were to be kept intact, then the domestic "criticism or polemics" would have to stop. Even with a loyal home front the army could hold out only for a few more days. . . . He, Hindenburg and

> "every other honorable soldier" were agreed that if the attacks on the Kaiser did not cease, then the "fate of the army (was) sealed; it will break in pieces. And the wild beast will break out in the bands of irregular soldiery pouring back into their native land."

"It will be saving the German Empire from internal disintegration and dissolution, if the structure of the Army remains firm, if its desire for a common Fatherland is unweakened and its spirit held to obedience."[15]

Like his predecessor, Groener wanted to keep his army intact, but he no longer planned to use it against the foreign enemy; that defeat was already accepted. He valued a disciplined army as an instrument for national stability at a time of crisis. That army must help to protect, even influence, an

organic German change in the crucible of defeat.  That army
must screen out, and uproot, the Bolshevik threat to central
Europe.  This was its mission and service to the continuing
German interest.

After Groener's report, the war council heard from Haussmann concerning the naval revolt in Kiel.  That rebellion was
already under the direction of a Workers' and Sailors' Soviet.
Its leaders demanded abdication and amnesty.  Haussmann
recommended that they be conciliated, but the council refused
and undertook to isolate the city from outside road and rail
communication.  Such news confronted Groener with the very
domestic dissolution he feared most.  Unlike the council,
Groener did not think the Kiel rebellion could be localized.
The public temper was much too strained to forego demonstration against that authority which had promised, and exacted
so much and had disillusioned so many.  It would be sparked
into planless and manipulated protest.  Local military police
would not prevail for the entire movement was against the authority of the uniform.  Successful containment would require
sizeable troop contingents.  And even if they were available,
which they were not, Groener was sure that after four years
of trial and comradeship, "field grey would not shoot against
field grey." He expected the Kiel rebellion to jump its flimsy
barrier into nearby cities and then spread throughout the nation.  Not Kiel, but the army in the west, faced early isolation.

When he arrived in Berlin, Groener was informed at the
railroad station that the American drive toward Sedan was ac-
celerating and that key position would soon be gone.  Demanding unity at home, he heard of revolution.  And probably
he did, as Haussmann said, "change his estimate of the front's
capacity to resist overnight." On the morning of November 6,
Groener told Prince Max that there must be an armistice in
three days.  Diplomatic negotiations were too slow; emissaries
would have to cross the line with the white flag.  As he explained to the later council,

> "I too hoped that we could hold eight to ten days un-
> til we could settle in our new line.  After being in-
> formed of what has since happened in Kiel, Tyrol
> and to home morale, especially in Bavaria with its
> very serious political consequences, I have become

convinced that we must take the step, as painful
as it is, and ask Foch. "

Before leaving the capital, Groener met with Social Democratic leaders.   The government was relying on them to retain
control of the masses and to preserve monarchism.  It arranged
the meeting in the hope that they might persuade Groener's en-
listment in the abdication campaign.  The labor leaders asked
their favorite general to help unseat the Kaiser and thereby relieve revolutionary pressure. Although republicans in principle,
they were willing to defend the Empire from revolution, but
without a crown change they would lose the masses to Bolshevik leadership. Groener understood and refused. He told them
the army and the Kaiser belonged together.   After all these
years the Kaiser could not simply say "I abdicate. "

As these troubled patriots appealed and parried, Scheidemann entered to report excitedly that the revolution had jumped
from Kiel to Hamburg and Hanover; "the abdication is now no
longer a matter for discussion, the revolution is on the march."
The effort to localize the Kiel uprising failed and now it was
fanning into the nation.

The stolid Ebert lost neither nerve nor patience. He turned
to Groener, "Once more, General, I urgently advise you to take
the last opportunity to save the monarchy by helping to bring
about the regency of one of the royal princes." The group
pressed anxiously around Groener.   They warned that unless
he helped secure abdication, Germany faced catastrophe, but
the soldier did not strike his Spa colors. Abdication was out
of the question, he said, and the princes were already on rec -
ord against the regency idea.   It was enough for Ebert.

" Under those circumstances further discussion is su-
perfluous.  Now things must run their course.  We
thank you, excellency, for the frank discussion and
we shall always remember with pleasure our coopera-
tive work with you during the war.  From now on our
paths go different ways. Who knows if we shall see
one another again. "

As the labor leaders filed out, Colonel Haeften remarked to
Groener, "That means revolution.  These leaders no longer

have the masses in hand."[16]

These men obviously felt themselves to be in the presence of a great historical moment. Their own Empire was dying and the great Russian revolution in the east was visible and frightening to all of them. There, such beginnings had ramified into a cataclysmic social earthquake. Every decision in Berlin or Spa might be the crucial determinant for a sane adjustment or a wild reaction.

Groener returned to Spa with a clear, if troubled, heart. Despite the voice of reality within himself, he did not betray the Kaiser in absentia. Later he would remember the rejection of Ebert's plea as his biggest mistake and guilt in the collapse, but that was mere speculative and agonizing retrospect. His disavowal of the Kaiser in Berlin might have agitated the army into its own civil war, and quiet collusion with the Berlin leaders also had its dubious prospects. An earlier decision against the ruler might have developed its own dangerous repercussions. Maybe a certain helpless patience in those days was not so fatal. A quiet transition depended more on his cooperation than on timing or tactic, and in a few days the withering fruit would drop by itself.

Back at Spa, Groener watched and planned, meditating on ways to preserve the old army in the new Germany. The armistice delegation came west on the same train with him and the front problem was resolving itself. Groener swung his attention toward his own country, especially to the Rhine, which was a critical transportation barrier in any large scale evacuation or demobilization. Millions of riflemen must be canalized quickly and efficiently into quiescent, responsible family life. Traffic congestion there would expose impatient, calloused veterans to the army-baiting agitation of demagogue egalitarians. Groener dispatched a communications officer to observe and report on revolutionary conditions in the key rail city of Cologne. He also set up a special map of his rear echelon network in order to keep close watch on the security of his supply lines. He and his staff discussed the formation of anti-revolutionary free corps to engage revolution in Germany, assert the German interest in the east and generally give professional, patriotic occupation to the expected officer surplus. Anticipating the appearance of soldiers' councils in the ranks and hoping to neutralize their revolutionary effect,

he considered their creation by command. In a few days officers from the Imperial army would pick their own soldiers'
councils. This was revolution a la General Staff.

Although planning for the future, Groener was yet unresolved about the Kaiser question. It was the unavoidable
hurdle for changing Germany and unless the army rejected
William there was little chance of his elimination without a
civil war. Already knee-deep in a rising tide of revolution on
November 8, the government again dispatched a request for
abdication. Its liaison men in Spa, Hintze and Gruenau, prepared to deliver the petition to the Kaiser and they asked
Groener to join them. Again he refused. He had repeatedly
advised Hindenburg that the combat soldier would not fight for
the Kaiser in civil war. Beyond such suggestive information
he could not go; he could not break away from his old commander.[17] And as yet Hindenburg stood stolidly with his Kaiser
against unexplainable destiny. A proclamation to the army on
November 6 reminded his men of their sacred obligation,

"Every member of the army has sworn an oath of loyalty to the Kaiser and for it there is no Kaiser question.
Come what may the army will honor its oath. The
only justification necessary is unshakeable conviction."

But the large majority of his countrymen no longer possessed
such "unshakeable conviction" in Hohenzollern leadership,
and they were hardly ready to sacrifice themselves for their
service oath. These were no longer Nibelungen days.

The revolution assumed national scope on November 8.
Major cities everywhere fell into the hands of soldiers' and
citizens' committees and the government tabulated sweeping
"red" success. The capital poised in uneasy quiet as it a-
waited response to a Majority Socialist ultimatum for abdication. Ebert's party had to jettison the Kaiser in order to retain
leadership of the street public. Given abdication it hoped to
"guarantee a favorable development of the situation." Conservative socialism was about to seize authority in defense
of itself and in defense of German bourgeois society.

The revolution delivered the coup de grace to the stricken
armies on the front. Every major rail hub in the west passed
into rebel hands and Groener expected the Rhine bridges to

follow suit. His forces had supplies for half a week and were hopelessly wedged between foreign and domestic foe. They could not disengage Allied pressure until the armistice was signed and for the moment, limitation of the revolution depended on moderates at home. To all but a few it seemed the military had no choice but to tolerate Majority Socialist leadership and contingent political alterations. But the obdurate few still commanded at Spa.

On this frightening day of revolution Prince Max desperately tried for abdication. By telegram and telephone he explained to William that civil war and possible better peace terms hinged on such action. Ebert's faction could contain Bolshevism, but not without this symbol of punishment and of fundamental change. The Kaiser, however, felt secure with his army and rejected the pleas from Berlin. With amazing nerve he ordered Groener to prepare an operation for the recovery of authority between Aachen and Cologne. It was to regain control of the Rhine line and begin the march to Berlin. "The Kaiser," mused Groener later, "still reckoned with a temporarily ugly mood in Germany which would vanish with his appearance."

The sorely perplexed Groener continued in duty and he prepared an elite division for the Aachen-Cologne project. To complement this initial test of dynastic strength he also decided to sound the spirit of the combat soldier. Was the rank and file committed to the Kaiser against a revolutionary home front? Groener thought not but it was time for substantiation. Each army was instructed, without further explanation, to send five regimental commanders to Spa. Apparently the order was deliberately brief so higher echelon might not suspect and obstruct. Groener wanted no misrepresentation. "We needed," he explained, "the judgment of those leaders who lived in direct contact with the troops." He also polled his headquarters for its estimate of the army's solidarity with the Kaiser.

Events soon confirmed Groener's doubts. Instead of spearheading a Hohenzollern recovery, the elite division mutinied and its "field grey" trooped for home. The spirit of revolt was infecting the army and its relationship to the Kaiser demanded clarification. That night Groener's report to Hindenburg and Plessen indirectly conveyed his conclusion in the Kaiser question. He gave an unsparing account of combat

exhaustion and logistical paralysis. The army had neither reserves nor supply system; it did not even have a supporting
state.  Everywhere revolutionary success was established or
impending and obviously beyond Imperial correction.  The mutiny of that day reflected the unreliability of the troops.  The
cause was lost and they wanted peace and life.  Effective police action by the army was not immediately possible; it would
be folly to send cynical,  exhausted war units against the
catching slogans of revolution. The disobedient element would
prevail and start a landslide to complete military disintegration and revolutionary triumph.  Dissolution of the war army
was prerequisite to the selective construction of a counter-
revolutionary corps.  Such reorganization was impossible without a few weeks time and a peaceful return to Germany.

Groener's analysis implied the necessity for abdication.
Plessen understood and resisted.  It seemed preposterous that
the great German army should capitulate to a handful of trai-
terous rascals. A few units, dispatched to key points, would
quickly restore order.  The Aachen–Cologne project was the
beginning of such corrective action and it must be undertaken.
The monarchy must not run down its colors without a fight.
Groener shared Plessen's sentiments but not his conclusions
and he stood by his depressing facts and interpretation.  The
army was helpless and momentarily unreliable; it was physi-
cally and spiritually incapable of disciplining the home front.

Hindenburg listened in silence as the unbending honor
and class interest of the old vassal dueled with the more realistic preservation tactics of the younger bourgeois.  The
stolid field marshal accepted the analysis of his executive
officer and the two decided to report the impossibility of coun-
terrevolution to the Kaiser the following morning.  The dye was
cast at Spa.  The army could choose either civil war or subordination to domestic developments which were abandoning
the Kaiser. Groener said nothing of abdication to Plessen but
he grimly defined and stubbornly opposed the alternative of
civil war.  His logic received Hindenburg's sanction and
thenceforth represented the High Command. It chose the continuity of nation and army to untimely, undeserving, all-
destroying counter-revolution.

Later that evening Groener received a telephone call from
Payer.  The truce with Berlin's labor was expiring and Payer

asked Groener for help in securing abdication. From the en-
suing conversation, Payer got the impression that Groener was
finally willing to abandon the Kaiser, but the general was still
resolved that William affirm that decision himself. Such a
voluntary abdication was needed in order to cushion the de-
moralization of the aristocratic officers' corps.[18]

On the morning of November 9 the Kaiser awaited his generals in the garden of his villa. They were to report on the
progress of the Aachen-Cologne project. Another urgent abdication telegram from Berlin had been delivered and disregarded.
William was now serenely resolved to stay in command and
fight his way back to Berlin if necessary. As they waited, he
and his aides discussed the revolution and its Bolshevik challenge, confident that Imperial action would soon turn the tide.
Apparently neither Hindenburg nor Plessen had previewed the
Kaiser on the scheduled briefing.

Hindenburg and Groener met again that morning to confirm
their information and conclusion. They also read telegrams
from Berlin which reported public and government sentiment for
abdication. They were approached by Hintze who once more
asked for help in implementing such action. Their response
must have been satisfactory for he telephoned Berlin that the
High Command was about to confess the army's helplessness
and disloyalty to the Kaiser. The listening official in Berlin
remarked that such a report would make abdication unavoidable.
Hintze said nothing. The Berlin official immediately called
Ebert in order to stop the planned labor demonstration with his
abdication promise, but it was too late. William's problem
children, the proletariat, already were in the streets and the
overthrow of Imperial authority was under way.

At Spa the commanding pair moved toward the painful ren-
dezvous. En route Hindenburg stopped to welcome and brief
the regimental commanders who were so hastily assembled by
Groener's veiled order. Numb with cold, fatigue and despon-
dency, they clustered around their venerated patriarch for explanation. He told them they were to give account of the
soldiers' unwillingness to fight with the Kaiser against the
home front. He also gave a digest of Groener's evening report,
underlining the bleak supply situation and warning that successful action would entail a three-week drive to Berlin.

Having explained the problem to the lower echelons,

Hindenburg resumed course with Groener and Plessen. The tall, spare Prussian dabbed his eyes; the stock Wuerttemberger showed no emotion. He had given warning earlier than most and been stigmatized for it by the selfsame Plessen. Already numbed by multiple frustration, Groener's passionate Schlieffen soul had sustained the psychological shock of defeat months before. Now, resigned and impassive, he grasped ugly reality with firm courage to present it where it had not been presented before.

At the briefing Hindenburg quickly excused himself. The old soldier stood night watch at the bier of William I and he could not read sentence on the last Hohenzollern. As a Prus - sian officer he pleaded inability to say what had to be said; he would rather resign than report the army's disloyalty. The theme was set. "We shall see, " parried the Kaiser and eyes turned to the executive.

Groener was slightly surprised but hardly unsettled. His analysis was made and he did not mind repeating it, but the Wuerttemberger was determined to stand clear of the abdica- tion decision which devolved more properly on William and his Prussian advisors. He was not inclined to assume respon- sibility for the historical decision at hand and was quite will- ing to let events set their own imperative. Once more he ex- plained the army's hopeless situation, sparing no evidence and insinuating no conclusion. He claimed confirming support from Hindenburg and from every section chief in Headquarters.

The Groener report requested cancellation of the Aachen- Cologne operation and implied abandonment of the Kaiser. The defendant ruler hoped for disagreement and asked Count Schu- lenburg for his view. This forceful and class-confident junker echoed and fortified the earlier protest of Plessen. He con- sidered the Groener analysis unjustifiably.black. Quick troop consignments into the nation would restore order, especially if armed with a stirring slogan to rekindle the patriotism of army and public. The response would be unquestionable if naval and revolutionary treachery against the heroic front soldier were properly exposed. The heavy autumn fighting demonstrated that the men were still "firmly in hand." Mo- mentarily, of course, the prospect of armistice suspended all will to fight either foreign or domestic foe, but a ten-day rest would revive their Imperial loyalty, even against the Rhine.

The food situation was bad but they always could draw on rich Belgium.

Groener needed support and he got it. Commander in Chief Hindenburg upheld the validity of his executive's analysis. He and Groener expressed sympathy and understanding for the Schulenburg reaction but adhered to more pessimistic realism. Supported by his superior, Groener then launched his rebuttal, exposing the contradiction between the call for immediate rest and immediate action. The most reliable troops were deeply engaged at the front. In view of evacuation problems they could not be re-deployed even within a ten-day period. In the meanwhile the revolutionaries would continue the reduction and seizure of Germany. Past combat strength was no proof of present resilience. The troop mutiny of the preceding day demonstrated the unfeasibility of counter-revolutionary action, even with elite war units. As for Belgium, it was barren after four years of war and was already being evacuated. Also, the Rhine operation would merely begin the drive to Berlin. Revolutionary strength and destruction would increase in the face of the Imperial challenge. The Kaiser's army was unwilling and unable to subdue the home front, and such an effort would only bring Germany to ruin.

The Hohenzollern swayed between the hope and despair of his generals. He of course leaned toward Schulenburg who still accepted the reality of Imperial authority, but the commanding pair persisted. Recapture of the home front was not possible. Its attempt would unleash a suicidal civil war in which they could assume no responsibility for the loyalty of the army and even the safety of the Kaiser. It was slight balm to hear Groener condemn the government for past laxity in counter-propaganda. The unspoken choice remained abdication or civil war. William shyed from either, treasuring both public welfare and dynastic destiny, but he finally stepped toward his fate and cancelled the Aachen-Cologne operation. He would not cause civil war, but he delayed the alternative by requesting a poll of his senior commanders in the field. He had to be sure; he would go only if they denied him the loyalty of the army.

Groener stepped back. His analysis was delivered and the counter-revolutionary operation was cancelled. Although still seeking rescue, the Kaiser finally seemed cognizant of his helplessness. Events in Spa and Berlin would continue to narrow and force the ultimate decision. Thinking his painful chore completed, Groener gladly slipped into the smaller discussion groups which formed in the garden. The facts were in; the decision was not his to make. But his withdrawal was to be merely an interlude and it served to raise him in even sharper prominence.

Cancellation of the Aachen-Cologne project admitted the inability of Imperial recovery. Schulenburg now tacked in continuing, tenacious defense of his liege lord and their way of life. He urged that William surrender only the German crown and return home as Prussian King in the safe escort of Schulenburg's loyal troops. Groener retorted that such dynastic manipulation was several weeks too late and now impossible against surging revolutionary sentiment which was directed against the very person of the Kaiser, but Schulenburg stiffened with his new idea and the Kaiser seemed receptive. Nationalist Groener then lost his cautious neutrality and self-restraint. He was "startled by this action" which forsook the unity of army and nation. His concern was not for Hohenzollern Prussia but for a united Germany. Confounded by "so much unreality," patience left him and he served notice on Schulenburg and the Kaiser, "The army will march home in peace and order under its leaders and commanding generals, but not under the command of Your Majesty, for it no longer stands behind Your Majesty."

Mutiny, pronounced by Groener and given mute confirmation by Hindenburg, was within Imperial earshot. The Kaiser's face darkened and he snapped at the offending speaker, "Excellency, my commanding generals will have to tell me that in writing." Groener stood alone in the silence of the garden, conscious of his irritation and exposure. He half expected to witness a suicide, or be shot down himself.

Schulenburg again opposed Groener's view and he pledged the loyalty of all the generals in his army group. His highest maxim seemed to be command and obedience in ultimate commitment to the Hohenzollern. In the face of national disintegration and front line exhaustion, he could still speak of his men as being "firmly in hand." Such words hardly did justice to their four years of sacrificing service and to the national problem of the moment. In fact, Schulenburg's commanding

officer, the Crown Prince, was already angrily upset by the
desertions and poor behavior of their own Fifth army. And
soon Schulenburg would be stung by another Groener heresy
and overwhelmed by a massive rebuttal from the trenches and
from Berlin's angry streets.

The group broke into smaller clusters and again the bourgeois realist crossed ideological swords with his junker colleagues. One of these expressed amazement at the developing
disloyalty of the officers. Had they not sworn an oath of
fealty to the war lord? Groener observed that in such moments
of personal and national strain, the terms war oath and war
lord were fictitious. Schulenburg who was told of this comment was sure that Groener did not know the "pulsebeat" of
the front soldier, who was dedicated to the Kaiser and inspired
by the "bible and the song book." Not too many armies in the
world would qualify for such description and certainly not the
battered German army of 1918.

Colonel Heye appeared next to report on troop morale as
represented by the assembled front commanders. They had
been asked two questions. Would the men fight with the Kaiser
against the revolution? Would they fight against Bolshevism
at all? Groener and Hindenburg were already worried about a
future which extended beyond the Kaiser. The response to
both questions was resoundingly negative and gave parliamentary expression to the exhausted apathy of the German army.
Only one of the thirty-nine officers polled thought the troops
would fight with the Kaiser in counter-revolution. That lone
optimist, incidentally, was not from Schulenburg's army group
which was represented by sixteen delegates of whom twelve
said no and four were uncertain. Not one of the thirty-nine
could give unconditional promise of help against Bolshevism.
Nineteen were uncertain and twelve thought the men would
fight against such a challenge after a few weeks of rest and
orientation.

Heye added a comment to his statistics,

"The troops still are loyal to Your Majesty but they
are tired and indifferent; they want only peace and
rest. At the moment they will not march against the
homeland, not even with Your Majesty at their head.
And they will not march against Bolshevism; they

want only armistice, the sooner the better."

Later critics of this poll said that the assembled commanders had travelled all night and were naturally grim, tired,
and depressed. Given some rest and refreshment they might
have viewed the situation with more optimism. Groener's discreet communication with the lower command echelons has
also been frowned on. This was dubious military procedure.
Why did he not ask the commanding generals about army morale, said one critic. They would have given him an entirely
different answer. Groener went to the troop commanders because he wanted information about the men on the front. He
had enough realistic experience and intelligence to realize
that the army generals might not be too intimate, or even too
honest, with the mood of the front. Schulenburg and the Crown
Prince gave excellent illustration of higher echelon hauteur
and incomprehension. And if the assembled troop commanders
were cold and tired after an over-night train ride, maybe their
vote was thereby even more intimately realistic and representative. The men on the front were tired too and they were not
sleeping in relatively snug railroad cars. And if Groener's
poll was unusual to military procedure, how should one rate
the behavior of the men it offended? Was their stubborn and
selfish control of German life in keeping with the larger pro-
prieties of national interest and welfare?

The distraught Kaiser's fate seemed clear enough after the
Heye report but he explored it a step further. He asked, "Will
the army march home in order without me? Groener thinks yes;
Schulenburg no." Again Heye's answer hurt,

"The troops will march home in order under their generals alone and in this respect they still are in the
hands of their leaders. And they extend joyous welcome to His Majesty if he wants to come along. But
the army wants to fight no more, neither at the front
nor at home."

The survey of the troop commanders was a crushing blow, supporting Groener and relieving his isolation. His pessimism
received additional substantiation from Berlin.

After Hintze's morning phone call, government officials

in Berlin waited anxiously for the culmination and they maintained pressure with reports of mounting disorder. The workers were in the streets and key guard units joined the demonstrators. There was gunfire and bloodshed, but the city was hardly "flowing in blood" as the government reported to Spa. Hintze unsuccessfully tried to speak with Prince Max and finally checked with army headquarters in Berlin. That office modified the picture of violence but did confess inability to control the city. This confirmation reached the Kaiser directly after the Heye report and only minutes before another bid for abdication from Prince Max, which demanded action in minutes, not hours. This confluence of bad news from army, people, and government climaxed the Kaiser's agony. He decided to advise Berlin of pending abdication of the German, not the Prussian, crown. The Schulenburg straw was still being clutched but without loyal soldiers all royal strategy was mere delusion and the Prussian capital hardly qualified as a haven for continuing Hohenzollern rule.

The declaration drawn up by the Kaiser's advisers expressed readiness to abdicate the German crown alone. Hintze read it to Berlin and barely gained audience. The listening party interjected protest to the partial abdication move and, after allowing Hintze to finish, dropped its own bombshell. He read a governmental proclamation which already had been released to a national news agency. It began,

> "The Kaiser and King has resolved to renounce the throne. The Chancellor will remain in office until those questions are settled which relate to the Kaiser's abdication, to the crown waiver of the German and Prussian crown prince and to the installation of the regency."

Prince Max finally deposed his own relative in a last effort to preserve monarchism and the public order. Not many minutes later Spa heard that Scheidemann had announced the republic.

On receiving the abdication news, the Kaiser's shock at first was matched by militant anger. "Treason, shameless, outrageous treason," he cried and began to fill telegram blanks with his denial of the Berlin pronouncements. He assured his son and Schulenburg that he would stay as King of Prussia and these two again urged counter-revolution. But William rejected the idea of civil war and the Groener-Hindenburg pair did not forget to remind him that Berlin developments were beyond army control.  The Marshal explained rather plaintively that he could not allow His Majesty to be seized and judged by street mobs.  The court then decided on a written protest a-gainst the Berlin coup, to be made public at a later date. The Kaiser was no stronger than his army; both were isolated and helpless. In this final spasm of life and death it was Hinden-burg who most inflexibly precluded remedy.  His words were deferential but his solidarity with the Groener position was not.    It  was  he  who  finally  recommended  Holland  as  a sanctuary. [19]

The spotlight of history had fixed on Groener and debate released his tongue and judgments. After rejecting the Imperial sanctities he retired to unobtrusive observation.  Heye and the Berlin bulletins showed he had not misgauged the sentiment of his army and people.  He and other liquidation associates calculated the consequences of dynastic will and heeded their responsibility to the nation. Suicidal self-destruction, in the presence of Allied armies and Bolshevik opportunists, may well have been averted. The fate and lesson of 1945 had been avoided. [20]

# NOTES TO THE TEXT

## Chapter One

[1] For the Wuerttemberg background see Gustav Ruemelin, Reden und Aufsaetze (Frieburg, 1894), III, 384; Albert Schaeffle, Aus meinem Leben (Berlin, 1905), I, 134; Veit Valentin, Die Geschichte der deutschen Revolution von 1848/49 (Berlin, 1931), II, 499; Adolf Rapp, Die oeffentliche Meinung in Wuerttemberg von 1866 bis zu den Zollparlamentswahlen, Mai 1868 (Stuttgart, 1907), 53.

[2] Alfred Schlieffen, Briefe, ed. by E. Kessel (Goettingen, 1958), 254. See also Gerhard Ritter, Staatskunst und Kriegshandwerk, (Munich, 1960), II, 123.

[3] The Papers of General William Groener (in microfilm), roll IV, piece 17. Hereafter referred to as Groener Papers. See also Wilhelm Groener, Lebenserinnerungen, ed. by F. H. von Gaertringen (Goettingen, 1957), 43f.

[4] Eberhard Kessel, Moltke (Stuttgart, 1957), 697ff. See also Franz Endres, The Social Structure and Corresponding Ideologies of the German Officers' Corps (New York, 1937), 6; Robert von Mohl, Lebenserinnerungen (Leipzig, 1902), II, 163; Friedrich Naumann, Demokratie und Kaisertum (Berlin, 1904), 211.

[4] As reported in Graf Carl von Wedel, Zwischen Kaiser und Kanzel, ed. by E. v. Wedel (Leipzig, 1943), 125. See also Gerhard A. Ritter, Die Arbeiterbewegung im Wilhelminischen Reich (Berlin, 1959), 23-40.

[6] William II was reported to have said of the constitution, "Die Verfassung habe ich nie gelesen und kenne sie nicht." He wanted "eine starke Regierung, die ohne Reichstag wirtschaften

kann." Ritter, Staatskunst, II, 157, 165.

[7] Schlieffen, Briefe, 284, and Hohenlohe-Schillingsfuerst, Denkwuerdigkeiten der Reichskanzlerzeit, ed. by K.A. von Mueller (Berlin, 1931), 534.

[8] Tim Klein, ed., Der Kanzler; Otto von Bismarck in seinen Briefen, Reden und Erinnerungen (Munich, 1915), 172, and Elard von Oldenburg-Januschau, Erinnerungen (Leipzig, 1936), 99, 110. See also General Oberst Helmuth von Moltke, Erinnerungen, Briefe, Dokumente 1877-1916, ed. by E. von Moltke (Stuttgart, 1922), 143.

[9] Hans-Guenter Zmarzlik, Bethmann Hollweg als Reichskanzler, 1909-1914 (Duesseldorf, 1957), 100-125. See also Das Reichsarchiv, "Kriegsruestung und Kriegswirtschaft," Der Weltkrieg 1914 bis 1918 (Berlin, 1928), II, 121ff, and Ritter, Staatskunst, II, 167ff.

[10] Groener Papers, XVI, piece 149.

[11] Groener might well be understood as one of those new German nationalists who placed the interest of the state above all regional or class sentiment. Max is described as an outstanding example of such "National-egoismus" in Wolfgang J. Mommsen, Max Weber und die Deutsche Politik, 1890-1920 (Tuebingen, 1959), 42.

## Chapter Two

[1] Ritter, Staatskunst, I, 60-90, 269. The outstanding work on the relationship between the modern German state and army. For an excellent sketch of the German shift from idealism to materialism see also Walther Hofer, Geschichte zwischen Philosophie und Politik (Basel, 1956), 47-71.

[2] Rudolf Schmidt-Bueckeburg, Das Militaerkabinett der Preussischen Koenige und Deutschen Kaiser (Berlin, 1933), 214.

[3] Geleralfeldmarschall Graf Helmuth von Moltke, Gesammeltke Schriften (Berlin, 1892), V, 194.

[4] Moltke's strategic concepts are given documentary presentation in Graf Moltke, "Die deutschen Aufmarschplaene 1871-1890," Forschungen und Darstellungen aus dem Reichsarchiv

(Berlin, 1929). See also Kessel, _Moltke_, 625-650.

[5] Alfred von Schlieffen, _Gesammelte Schriften_ (Berlin, 1913), II, 451. See also Ritter, _Staatskunst_, II, 115-282.

[6] Gerhard Ritter, _Der Schlieffenplan_ (Munich, 1956), 43. The best analysis of the Schlieffen Plan with documentary presentation of the classic memorandum and its related fragments.

[7] Ritter, _Schlieffenplan_, 96f, and Graf Hutten-Czapski, _Sechzig Jahre Politik und Gesellschaft_ (Berlin, 1936), 371ff.

[8] For information on this point see Das Deutsche Auswaertige Amt, _Die Grosse Politik der Europaeischen Kabinette 1871-1914_ (Berlin, 1925), XIX, part 2, 479f; Karl von Einem, _Erinnerungen eines Soldaten_ (Leipzig, 1933), 111-115; Ritter, _Schlieffenplan_, 102-119.

[9] Ritter, _Staatskunst_, II, 239-281, and _Schlieffenplan_, 141-200.

[10] _Groener Papers_, XVIII, piece 168. As Groener warned at the beginning of his report, "Es wird viel zu wenig darueber nachgedacht, wie schwierig die Nutzbarmachung der Vorraete des Landes ist, wie besonders bei einem laengeren, die Entscheidung suchenden, unaufhaltsamen Vormarsch die Heranschaffung der Vorraete des Landes an die Marschstraessen mit der Schnelligkeit der Vorwaertsbewegung kaum Schritt halten kann."

[11] Herman von Kuhl, _Der deutsche Generalstab_ (Berlin, 1920), 169f, and Wolfgang Foerster, _Aus der Gedankenwerkstatt des deutschen Generalstabes_ (Berlin, 1921), 38. Compare a statement by the older Moltke in 1870, "Wir suchen in diesem Krieg die feindliche Armee auf, das ist das strategische Objekt fuer uns; geht die feindliche Armee nach Belgien, so suchen wir sie dort auf..." As cited in Generaloberst von Seeckt, _Moltke_, (Berlin, 1931), 128.

[12] Moltke, _Erinnerungen_, 245f. See also the very instructive study by Hermann Gackenholz which concludes that Moltke valued the Schlieffen Plan only in case the French army remained defensive. This he did not expect after 1905 and he modified the operation. Gackenholz, _Entscheidung in Lothringen 1914_, 19ff.

[13] Zmarzlik, _Bethmann Hollweg_, 101-140, and _Verhandlungen_

des Reichstags (Berlin, 1913), Vol. 291, 6282c.

[14] Reichsarchiv, Kriegsruestung, II, 57, 178ff. As War Minister Heeringen told Moltke in 1913, "Ich halte eine Vergroesserung der preussischen Armee um fast ein Sechstel ihres Bestandes fuer eine so einschneidende Massnahme, dass eingehend erwogen werden muss, ob nicht ihr innerer Gehalt... wesentlich darunter leidet. Ohne ein Hineingreifen in fuer die Ergaenzung des Offizierkorps wenig geeignete Kreise, das, von anderen Gefahren abgesehen, dadurch der Demokratisierung ausgesetzt waere,..."

[15] Carl E. Schorske, German Social Democracy, 1905-1917 (Cambridge, 1955), 60-85.

[16] A. von Tirpitz, Politische Dokumente (Berlin, 1924), 160. Opinion rendered at a crown council held on June 3, 1909.

[17] Groener Papers, XIII, piece 132.

[18] Groener, Einnerungen, 131-140, and Groener Papers, XIX, pieces 172-178.

[19] Reichsarchiv, Kriegsruestung, II, 66f, 76ff, 87, 92f, 184f, 192f.

[20] Reichsarchiv, Kriegsruestung, II, 349.

## Chapter Three

[1] Mommsen, Max Weber, 158. In a prophetic letter of December 31, 1889, Weber wrote, "Wenn nur der junge Kaiser erst Konsistenz gewonnen haben wird! Diese boulangistisch-bonapartistische Art von Kundgebungen sind doch nachgerade unerwuenscht. Man hat den Eindruck, als saesse man in einem Eisenbahnzuge von grosser Fahrgeschwindigkeit, waere aber im Zweifel, ob auch die naechste Weiche richtig gestellt werden wuerde."

[2] The entire question of the Kaiser's simple and tasteless authoritarianism is illustrated in Reichsarchiv, Kriegsruestung, II, 21, 38; Kessel, Moltke, 746; Tirpitz, Politische Dokumente, 332. He could tell his generals of Bismarck, "Er verweigert mir die Heeresfolge...will also nicht Ordre parieren! Er muss also fort.... Ich kann aber solche Minister nicht brauchen;

dieselben muessen mir vielmehr gehorchen." Such an attitude persisted and as a much older man, in 1913, the Kaiser could still inform the British government, "With respect to the intimation in the despatch, that Sir E. Grey could only conclude the agreement with the present Chancellor, Your Minister labours under an illusion. The Chancellor as well as the Foreign office are both purely officials of the Emperor. It is the Emperor, who gives them the directions as to which policy is to be pursued and they have to obey and follow his will."

[3] Friedrich Meinecke, Preussen und Deutschland im 19. und 20. Jahrhundert (Berlin, 1918), 34-40, 140.

[4] Mommsen, Weber, 45. "Nicht Frieden und Menschenglueck haben wir unseren Nachfahren mit auf den Weg zu geben," said Weber, "sondern den ewigen Kampf um die Erhaltung und Emporzuechtung unserer nationalen Art." And the legacy of Bismarch? "Er hinterliess seine Nation ohne alle und jede politische Erziehung, tief unter dem Niveau, welches sie in dieser Hinsicht zwanzig Jahre vorher bereits erreicht hatte. Und vor allem eine Nation ohne allen und jeden politischen Willen, gewohnt, das der grosse Staatsmann an ihrer Spirze fuer sie die Politik schon besorgen werde."

[5] Meinecke, Nach der Revolution, 44.

[6] Meinecke, Weltbuergertum und Nationalstaat (Berlin, 1915), 513.

[7] Karl Kautsky, Max Montgelas and Wilhelm Schuecking, ed., Die deutschen Dokumente zum Kriegsausbruch (Berlin, 1919), I, 98 and II, 122f. Gerhard Ritter said, "Aus reiner Furcht, ein paar Tage, veilleicht auch nur ein paar Studen zu spaet zu kommen, glaubte der Generalstab und damit auch die deutsche Regierung sich genoetigt, das Odium des Angreifers und Friedensbrechers auf sich zu laden." Gerhard Ritter, Lebendige Vergangenheit (Munich, 1958), 177.

[8] Groener's opinion on this mobilization problem expressed to General von Kuhl in a letter of December 28, 1922. Groener Papers, VIII, piece 34-1. Also repeated in Groener, Erinnerungen, 145f.

[9] Groener, Erinnerungen, 145, and Das Reichsarchiv, Das

deutsche Feldeisenbahnwesen (Berlin, 1928), 30-50.

[10] Reichsarchiv, Feldeisenbahnwesen, 59f, and Military Operations of Belgium, ed. by the Commander-in-Chief of the Belgian Army (London, 1915), 5. Special thanks are also due the Historical Section of the Belgian Ministry of National Defense, which graciously furnished me with information about those first days of invasion.

[11] French demolition orders were given but apparently the problem of proper timing and the lack of sufficient engineering personnel compounded the general confusion of crisis and withdrawal. See Les Armées Françaises dans La Grande Guerre (Paris, 1925), Tome Premier, II, 15f; A. Marchand, Les chemins de fer de l'est et la guerre de 1914-1918 (Paris, 1924), 12-28; D. Noce, Strategic Demolitions of Railroads in Front of the German Right Wing (Washington, 1940), 6-9.

[12] Reichsarchiv, Feldeisenbahnwesen, 90-100, and Generals von Kuhl and Bergmann, Movements and Supply of the German First Army during August and September 1914 (Fort Leavenworth, 1929), 40f, 112, 116f, 214.

[13] Marchand, Les chemins de fer, 296, and Les Armées Françaises, Tome Premier, III, 11ff.

[14] H. Baur, Deutsche Eisenbahnen im Weltkrieg 1914-1918 (Stuttgart, 1927), 16. See also Reichsarchiv, Der Weltkrieg 1914-1918 (Berlin, 1925), IV, 1-31; A. von Kluck, Der Marsch auf Paris und die Marneschlacht 1914 (Berlin, 1920), 95; Hermann von Kuhl, Der Marnefeldzug 1914 (Berlin, 1921), 85-120.

[15] Mueller-Loebnitz, "Die Sendung des Oberstleutnants Hentsch," Forschungen und Darstellungen aus dem Reichsarchiv (Berlin, 1922), 20-30. Moltke's performance stood judged by one of his own prewar lectures: If the parts of an army "follow their own separate purposes, which no longer correspond to the effort of the common action, then the High Command has lost its reins, it has not understood how to bring the necessary unity into the movements and battles of the single groups." Wolfgang Foerster, Graf Schlieffen und der Weltkrieg (Berlin, 1925), 15f.

[16] Groener Papers, III, piece 13-1, and Moltke, Erinnerungen, 384f.

[17] Reichsarchiv, Der Weltkrieg, IV, 517. See also a letter from the editor of the official German war history work to Groener, July 7, 1920, in which Haerfen expresses the consensus doubt "dass das deutsche Westheer zur Ausnuetzung eines etwaigen Erfolges wegen seiner schwierigen Nachschubverhaeltnisse gar nicht in der Lage gewesen sein wuerde." In Groener Papers, VIII. See also the diverse German views conveniently collected in E. Kaebisch, Streitfragen des Weltkrieges 1914-1918 (Stuttgart, 1924).

[18] Groener's war journal for this period in Groener Papers, III, piece 13-1. The correspondence with his wife in Groener Papers, V, piece 23, i-iv.

[19] This theme is best substantiated in Hans Gatzke, Germany's Drive to the West (Baltimore, 1950), 28, 117, 186ff, 250f.

[20] Groener Papers, XXV, piece 234-235, and III, 13-ii. "Die Aeusserung fuer den Reichskanzler ueber die Belgischen Bahnen ist mir noch nicht so gelungen," he wrote into his journal. "Angesichts der fehlenden Entscheidung...kann ueber die Belgische Frage eigentlich noch kein abschleissendes Urteil abgegeben werden."

[21] Theodore Heuss, Friedrich Naumann (Berlin, 1937), 439. See also Henry Cord Meyer, Mitteleuropa, in German Thought and Action, 1815-1945 (The Hague, 1955), 197f.

[22] Good samples of Groener's journal and correspondence available in his Erinnerungen, 526-546.

[23] Groener Papers, II, 383, and III, 13-ii.


Chapter Four

[1] Groener Papers, III, 13-ii. In referring to the wasteful use of the Sixth and Seventh armies in 1914, Groener wrote, "Davon geht die Kette aus, die unsere operative Freiheit mehr und mehr fesselt. Das ist die Frucht der boesen Tat, die fortzeugend Boeses muss gebaeren, das Fatum, dem wir nicht mehr entrinnen koennen, wenn uns nicht noch ein Gluecks zufall in den Schoss

faelit."

[2] Groener Papers, III, 13-iv, 13-v.

[3] "Er ist eben kein 'Staatsmann', der arme Kerl," Max could say of the Chancellor, "so wenig wie Moltke der Juengere ein Stratege war." Both men were personally comfortable for the Kaiser and thus entrusted with the German destiny. Mommsen, Max Weber, 249.

[4] Friedrich Meinecke, Probleme des Weltkriegs (Berlin, 1917), 11f, 40-70; Annelise Thimme, Hans Delbrueck als Kritiker der Wilhelminischen Epoche (Duesseldorf, 1955), 120-130; Gatzke, Germany's Drive to the West, 56, 60, 133.

[5] Groener Papers, II, 435, and III, 13-vi. This change of command, according to Arthur Rosenberg, "marked the downfall of the Bismarckian Empire and the beginning of the German Revolution." Arthur Rosenberg, The Birth of the German Republic (New York, 1931), 123.

[6] Reichsarchiv, Weltkrieg, XI, 443-461, and Klaus Epstein, Matthias Erzberger (Princeton, 1959), 155-165.

[7] Groener Papers, III, 13-vi. See also the interesting Meinecke article in the Frankfurther Zeitung, January 3, 1917, "Ein neues Autoritaetsband zwischen Staat und Massen muss geknuepft werden, und diese neue Autoritaet kann nur aus der freien und freudigen Gesinnung derer, die sie anerkennen sollen hervorgehen.... Denn nur diejenige Autoritaet gilt dem modernen Menschen noch als heilig und unverletzlich, die er in seinem Willen aufgenommen hat und innerlich miterzeugt.... Friedrich der Grosse, der im Rahmen des ancien regime das Junkertum pflegen musste, um ein festes Rueckgrat fuer sein bunt zusammengesetztes Heer zu haben, muesste heute die Massen pflegen, um das Einheits-und Massenheer zu haben, das ein siebenjaehriger Krieg im 20. Jahrhundert erfordert."

[8] Ralph Haswell Lutz, ed., Fall of the German Empire (Stanford, 1932), II, 141-198.

[9] Deutscher Reichstag, Die Ursachen des Deutschen Zusammenbruches im Jahre 1918 (Berlin, 1926), Vierte Reihe, VIII, 19f. "Der deutsche Generalstab Kaempfte gegen das englische Parlament, nicht etwa, weil in Deutschland der Militarismus

herrschte, sondern einfach deshalb, weil in Deutschland eine
dem englischen politischen Willen ebenbuertige politische
Macht, die die Anwendung der Gewalt Leitete, gehlte." Or as
Groener expressed it, "so wurde damals der Ruf nach der Mili-
taerdiktatur in irgendeiner Form laut, in dem festen, naiven
Glauben, dass unsere Militaers und vor allem der Generalstab
es schon 'schmeissen' werde." Erinnerungen, 338.

[10] Erich Ludendorff, ed., Urkunden der Obersten Heeresleitung
(Berlin, 1920), 63-80. See also Hindenburg's letter to Bethmann Hollweg on October 10, 1916, in Groener Papers, XX,
piece 192-i.

[11] As reported by Groener in a letter to the Reichsarchiv on
April 9, 1923. Groener Papers, XX, piece 192-i.

[12] As reported back to the High Command by Groener after the
first full day of discussion with other government officials on
October 29, 1916. "Es ist beabsichtigt, wenn das Ergebnis
der Montags-Nachmittagssitzung nicht meine zustimmung
findet, Abends 9 Uhl erneut die Minister zusammenzuberufen."
Groener Papers, XX, piece 192-i.

[13] Groener Papers, XX, piece 192-i. "...nur auf dem Boden
meines Vorschlages und unter Mitwirkung des Reichstags, der
unbedingt die Verantwortung mitzutragen hat,... ( Let the
Reichstag understand) dass wir nur mit Hilfe eines solchen
Gesetzes den Krieg gewinnen koennen." And in another letter
to Groener, "...wir koennen daher den Krieg nur gewinnen
wenn wir dem Heere soviel Kriegsgeraet zufuehren dass es
den feindlichen Armeen gleich stark gegenuebersteht...dieses
hoechstmas an Leistungen kann aber nur erreicht werden wenn
das gesamte Volk sich in den Dienst und nur in den Dienst der
Kriegswirtschaft und damit des Vaterlandes stellt.... schreiten
wir nicht zu einer schnellen und ganzen Loesung dieser Frage
so werden der Obersten Heeresleitung die Mittel zum Siege
entzogen."

[14] Groener Papers, XX, piece 192-i. As reported by Paul Um-
breit in the bulletin "Gemeinsame Arbeit der Behoerden und
der Gewerkschaften."

[15] Groener, Erinnerungen, 360, and Karl Helfferich, Der Weltkrieg (Berlin, 1919), II, 268f.

[16] Gatzke, Germany's Drive to the West, 144, 201.

[17] Letters from Ludendorff to Groener on January 26 and February 16, 1917. Groener Papers, XX, piece 192-i, 193. See also Groener, Erinnerungen, 356ff.

[18] The circumstances and conditions of Germany's internal collapse are best presented in Ursachen, Reihe Vier, IV-VII. Germany's radicals met with Russian Bolshevik leaders in Switzerland in 1915. It was decided to undertake "Massenaktionen" in order to stop the war and bring about social democracy. Germany's Independent Social Democrats accepted and propagated the idea of the mass strike. See especially Ursachen, Reihe Vier, V, 10-28.

[19] Lutz, Fall of German Empire, II, 224f.

[20] Ursachen, Reihe Vier, VI, 180f; Verhandlungen des Reichstags, Vol. 309, 3058ff, 3095, and Vol. 310, 3124, 3131, 3135-3141. See also the helpful new material presented in Heinrich Scheel, "Der Aprilstreik 1917 in Berlin," Revolutionaere Ereignisse und Probleme in Deutschland (Berlin, 1957). Scheel's documentary information appears reliable even though it serves a didactic, ideological purpose.

[21] Lutz, Fall of German Empire, II, 228f, and newspaper articles as arrayed in Groener Papers, XXI, piece 194.

[22] Gatzke, Germany's Drive to the West, 190, 250f; Epstein Matthias Erzberger, 170-200; Heuss, Friedrich Naumann, 469f.

[23] Groener, Erinnerungen, 368f, and Papers, XX, 192-ii. Groener wrote "Der Luegenbeutel" in the margin of the newspaper as he read that his memorandum had been denied in the Reichstag. Ludendorff queried him about its whereabouts in the Spring of 1918 and Groener referred him to the War Office files.

[24] Groener Papers, XX, piece 192-ii.

[25] As the Neue Zuercher Zeitung commented, "ihm war die Gabe richtiger Menschenbehandlung zu eigen." And Majority Socialist Scheidemann said, "General Groener, einer der verstaendigsten Offiziere ueberhaupt--Manchmal musste man annehmen, dass er der einzige hoehere Offizier war, der eine

Ahnung vom Leben, Leiden, Streben und Arbeiten des Volkes hatte--war abgesaegt worden." Groener Papers, XX, 192-ii, and Philipp Scheidemann, Memoiren eines Sozialdemokraten (Dresden, 1928), II, 60.

## Chapter Five

[1] Groener Papers, II, 13-viii, and Erinnerungen, 383. In a letter to his wife, "Dass im Gefolge eines solchen Weltkrieges, den man als groesste Umwaelzung staatlichen Lebens vielleicht wird buerteilen muessen, eine starke demokratische Welle ueber die Voelker geht, ist nicht zu verwundern....Die Hauptsache ist, dass die Monarchie bei uns obenauf bleibt. Wenn sie dies erreichen will, muss sie sich von der Welle tragen lassen und bestrebt sein, die Gesiter zu beherrschen. Das reine Verneinen und Entgegenstemmen gegen die natuerliche Entwicklung der Dinge koennte der Monarchie gefaehrlich werden.

[2] E. Ludendorff, Meine Kriegserinnerungen (Berlin, 1921), 472. Ernst Troeltsch wrote later that German leadership wanted only victory or defeat, "das Entweder-Oder." See Ernst Troeltsch, Spektator-Briefe, ed. by H. Baron (Tuebingen, 1924), 2.

[3] Groener's Ukraine tour of duty given military documentation in Papers, XXVII. See also his war journal and correspondence in III, 13-x and VI, piece 23, vi-ix. See further his Erinnerungen, 564-572, and John Reshetar, The Ukrainian Revolution (Princeton, 1952), 115-150.

[4] Lutz, Fall of the German Empire, II, 353ff, and Groener Papers, II, 555.

[5] Gustav Stresemann, Reden und Schriften (Dresden, 1926), I, 195, and Groener Papers, VI, piece 23, vi-ix.

[6] Groener, Erinnerungen, 412f, and Lutz, Fall of the German Empire, II, 460ff . For informed and divergent American analysis of the Ludendorff armistice tactics see Chester V. Easum, Half-Century of Conflict (New York, 1952), 66-72; Harry Rudin, Armistice 1918 (Yale, 1944), 54; A. Rosenberg, Birth of German Republic, 245f.

[6] For an interesting diagnosis of Ludendorff by a neutral col-

league, see Ludwig Beck, Studien, ed. by Hans Speidel (Stuttgart, 1955), 190-215. As Speidel said, "Sie zeigt die Gefahren einer Ein-Mann-Herrschaft, die Resignation erst des Staatsmannes, dann des militaerischen Fuehrers, aber auch den sittlichen Mut der damaligen Obersten Heeresleitung--trotz aller Fehler--, den Verlust des Krieges zu erkennen und daraus die Konsequenzen zu ziehen."

[7] Max von Baden, Erinnerungen Und Dokumente (Stuttgart, 1928), 340ff . See also Ursachen, Reihe Vier, VI, 48.

[8] Groener Papers, VI, piece 23, vi-ix.

[9] Reichskanzlei, Vorgeschichte des Waffenstillstandes (Berlin, 1919), 67-87, and Max, Erinnerungen, 419-452.

[10] "Die Sueddeutschen wuerden besser mit den Parlamentariern fertig, als die Preussen, hiess es." Groener was stung by the political overtones of his appointment although assured by Hindenburg it was based on military considerations. Groener Papers, I, 607.

[11] Walther Rathenau, Politische Briefe (Dresden, 1929), 205; Friedrich Meinecke, Erlebtes 1901-1919 (Berlin, 1947), 151. Or as Max Weber could say after the war: "... mit einer weltpolitischen Rolle Duerschlands ist es vorbei: die angelsaechsische Weltherrschaft... ist Tatsache. Sie ist hoechst unerfreulich, aber: viel Schlimmeres—die russische Knute!—haben wir abgewendet. Dieser Ruhm bleibt uns. Amerikas Weltherrschaft war so unabwendbar wie in der Antike, die Roms nach dem punischen Krieg. Hoffentlich bleibt es dabei, dass sie nicht mit Russland geteilt wird." Marianne Weber, Max Weber (Heidelberg, 1950), 685, and Max Weber, Gesammelte politische Schriften (Munich, 1921), 483f.

[12] Alfred Niemann, Revolution von Oben; Umsturz von Unten (Berlin, 1927), 123.

[13] The liaison man from Berlin was Hintze. His account in Niemann, Revolution von Oben, 367, checks with Groener, Papers, VIII, piece 34-i. Plessen's shocked response was, "Aber Sie wollen den Kaiser doch nicht in Lebensgefahr bringen!"

[14] Prince Max, Erinnerunge, 570f.

[15] National Chancellery, Preliminary History of the Armistice
(London, 1924), 137-143.  Even temporary German resistance
"would depend on whether the enemy could affect it material-
ly, especially on whether at one particular and very important
point, all attacks could be consistently repelled."  That point
was the American advance toward Sedan and the German defense
was being penetrated. See also Hans Herzfeld, Die deutsche
Sozialdemokratie und die Aufloesung der nationalen Einheitsfront im Weltkriege (Leipzig, 1928), 375.

[16] Prince Max, Erinnerungen, 591ff, and Groener Papers, I, 623.

[17] Niemann, Revolution von Oben, 377.  Groener told Hintze,
"Er habe dem Feldmarschall Wiederholt gesagt dass die Armee
zum Buergerkrieg wohl nicht zu haben sein wuerde, er koenne
aber den Feldmarschall nicht desavouieren."  In Groener's
words, the Kaiser "glaubte noch immer an eine voruebergehende
boese Stimmung in Deutschland, die mit seinem Erscheinen
verfliegen werde."  Groener Papers, II, 625.

[18] Friedrich Payer, Von Bethmann-Hollweg bis Ebert (Frankfurt/
Main, 1923), 159.  Apparently Payer conveyed no such anti-
cipation to Prince Max because the latter still believed Groener
to be obdurate. Prince Max, Erinnerungen, 625.

[19] All eye-witness accounts of the Spa council are from memory and they frequently diverge from, and contradict, one another.  Problematical, discriminating reconstruction is unavoidable. The official, royalist description of the scene, as
published on June 27, 1919, admittedly sought to portray the
scene in the Kaiser's favor.  Consisting of four eye-witness
accounts, it was carefully and loyally edited by Court Westarp.
Groener's views were not welcome and not officially included.
See Kuno Graf von Westarp, Das Ende der Monarchie (Berlin,
1952).  Groener insists that his rejection of the Kaiser followed the separatist maneuver of Schulenburg. He also main-
tains that his comment on "war oaths" was not heard by Hindenburg, the Kaiser and the Crown Prince, who were in another
cluster. The Crown Prince, incidentally, came late and missed
much of the action he so dramatically describes. Of Schulenburg and Plessen one can only agree with Walther Lambach's
statement, "Deutschland brach zusammen, ohne dass seine
herrschenden Kreise auch nur geahnt haetten, dass und in

welcher Weise sie selbst das Zerstoerungswerk vollbracht
haben." <u>Ursachen,</u> Reihe Vier, IV, 209. Groener was heart-
broken by the defeat of his Empire and a month later he would
refuse to give up his sword, insignia and medals to revolutionary delegates.  He also had his sacred "ideas" but they re-
volved around nation and army,  not around Prussia and the
Hohenzollerns.

# SELECTIVE BIBLIOGRAPHY

1. ## Unpublished Sources

   Groener, William. Papers. 27 rolls, microfilm. National Archives, Washington.

2. ## Published Documents

   Austria-Hungary. Ministerium des Aeussern. Diplomatische Aktenstuecke. Vienna, 1930.

   France. Ministere des affaires estrangeres. Documents diplomatiques francaises 1871-1914. Paris, 1929-1930.

   France. Les Armees Francaises dans La Grande Guerre. Paris, 1925.

   Germany. Auswaertiges Amt. Die Grosse Politik der Europaeischen Kabinette 1871-1914. Berlin, 1925.

   Germany. Reichskanzlei. Vorgeschichte des Waffenstillstandes. Berlin, 1919.

   Germany. Das Reichsarchiv. "Kriegsruestung und Kriegswirtschaft." Der Weltkrieg 1914 bis 1918. Berlin, 1930.

   Germany. Das Reichsarchiv. Der Weltkrieg, 1914-1918. Berlin, 1925.

   Germany. Untersuchungsausschuss. "Militaerische Ruestungen und Mobilmachungen." Zur Vorgeschichte des Weltkrieges. Berlin, 1921.

   Germany. Untersuchungsausschuss. Die Ursachen des

152

Deutschen Zusammenbruches im Jahre 1918. Berlin, 1926.

Germany. Verhandlungen des Reichstags. Berlin, series.

Great Britain. Gooch and Temperley. British Documents on the Origins of the War. London, 1926-1930.

Hoetzsch, Otto (ed.). Die Internationale Beziehungen im Zeitalter des Imperialismus. Berlin, 1931.

Kautsky, Montgelas and Schuecking (eds.). Die deutschen Dokumente zum Kriegsausbruch. Berlin, 1919.

Ludendorff, Erich (ed.). Urkunden der Obersten Heeresleitung. Berlin, 1920.

Lutz, Ralph Haswell (ed.). Fall of the German Empire 1914-1918. Stanford, 1932.

Moltke, Helmuth von. "Die deutschen Aufmarschplaene 1871-1890." Forschungen und Darstellungen aus dem Reichsarchiv. Berlin, 1929.

Schwertfeger, Bernhard (ed.). Zur Europaeischen Politik. Berlin, 1919.

Siebert, B. von (ed.). Diplomatische Aktenstuecke zur Geschichte der Ententepolitik der Vorkriegsjahre. Berlin, 1921.

Tirpitz, A. von (ed.). Der Aufbau der deutschen Weltmacht. Berlin, 1924.

3.  Letters, Journals and Memoirs

Baur, H. Deutsche Eisenbahner im Weltkrieg 1914-1918. Stuttgart, 1927.

Bauer, Max. Der grosse Krieg in Feld und Heimat. Tuebingen, 1921.

Baumgarten-Crusius. Die Marneschlacht 1914. Leipzig, 1914.

Bethmann-Hollweg, Theodore von. Betrachtungen zum Weltkriege. 2 vols. Berlin, 1921.

Bismarck, Otto von. Die politischen Reden, 14 vols.

Stuttgart, 1894.

Conrad von Hoetzendorff. Aus Meiner Dienstzeit 1906-1918. 6 vols. Vienna, 1923.

Delbrueck, Clemens von. Die Wirtschaftliche Mobilmachung in Deutschland 1914. Munich, 1924.

Ebert, Friedrich. Kaempfe und Ziele. Dresden, 1924.

Eckardtstein, Hermann von. Lebenserinnerungen und politische Denkwuerdigkeiten. 2 vols. Leipzig, 1920.

Einem, Karl von. Erinnerungen eines Soldaten. Leipzig, 1933.

Falkenhayn, Erich von. Die Oberste Heeresleitung 1914-1916. Berlin, 1920.

Goltz, Colmar von der. Denkwuerdigkeiten. Berlin, 1932.

Haussmann, Conrad. Schlaglichter, Reichstagsbriefe und Aufzeichnungen Frankfurt/Main, 1924.

Helfferich, Karl. Der Weltkrieg. 2 vols. Berlin, 1919.

Hindenburg, Paul von. Aus meinem Leben. Leipzig, 1920.

Hoffmann, Max von. The War of Lost Opportunities. London, 1926.

Hohenlohe-Schillingsfuerst, Chlodwig von. Denkwuerdigkeiten aus der Reichskanzlerzeit. Berlin, 1931.

Kluck, Alexander von. Wanderjahre - Kriege - Gestalten. Berlin, 1928.

Kluck, A. von. Der Marsch auf Paris und die Marneschlacht 1914. Berlin, 1920.

Kuhl, H. von. Der Marnefeldzug 1914. Berlin, 1921.

Generals von Kuhl and von Bergmann. Movements and Supply of the German First Army during August and September 1914. Fort Leavenworth, 1929.

Kuehlmann, Richard von. Gedanken ueber Deutschland. Leipzig, 1931.

Ludendorff, Erich. Mein militaerischer Werdegang.

Munich, 1937.

Ludendorff, Erich. Meine Kriegserinnerungen 1914-1918.
Berlin, 1921.

Max von Baden. Erinnerungen und Dokumente. Stuttgart,
1928.

Meinecke, Friedrich. Erlebtes 1862-1919. 2 vols. Berlin,
1941-1947.

Michaelis, George. Fuer Staat und Volk. Berlin, 1922.

Moltke, Helmuth von. Erinnerunge, Briefe, Dokumente
1877-1916. Stuttgart, 1922.

Moltke, Helmuth von (Sr.). Gesammelte Schriften. 7 vols.
Berlin, 1892.

Oldenbourg-Januschau, Elard von. Erinnerungen. Leipzig,
1936.

Payer, Friedrich. Von Bethmann-Hollweg bis Ebert. Frank-
furt/Main, 1923.

Rathenau, Walther. Politische Briefe. Dresden.

Rogge, Helmuth, ed. Holstein und Hohenlohe. Stuttgart,
1957.

Rupprecht von Bayern. Mein Kriegstagebuch. 3 vols.
Munich, 1929.

Scheidemann, Philipp. Der Zusammenbruch. Berlin, 1921.

Scheidemann, Philipp. Memoiren eines Sozialdemokraten.
2 vols. Dresden, 1928.

Schlieffen, Alfred von. Gesammelte Schriften. 2 vols.
Berlin, 1913.

Schlieffen, Alfred. Briefe, ed. by E. Kessel. Goettingen,
1958.

Seeckt, Generaloberst von. Gedanken eines Soldaten.
Leipzig, 1935.

Staabs, H. von. Aufmarsch nach zwei Fronten. Berlin, 1925.

Tappen. Bis zur Marne 1914. Berlin, 1920.

4. Monographs, Biographies, General Works

Barth, Emil. *Aus der Werkstatt der Revolution.* Berlin, 1919.

Beck, Ludwig. *Studien,* ed. by Hans Speidel. Stuttgart, 1955.

Bernstein, Eduard. *Die Deutsche Revolution.* Berlin, 1921.

Briethaupt, Wolfgang. *Volkesvergiftung 1914-1918.* Berlin, 1925.

Cochenhausen, Friedrich von. *Soldatische Fuehrer und Erzieher.* Hamburg, 1942.

Delbrueck, Hans. *Krieg und Politik.* Berlin, 1918.

Easum, Chester V. *Half-Century of Conflict.* New York, 1952.

Epstein, Klaus. *Matthias Erzberger.* Princeton, 1959.

Endres, Franz. *The Social Structure and Corresponding Ideologies of the German Officers' Corps.* New York, 1937.

Foerster, Wolfgang. *Aus der Gedankenwerkstatt des deutschen Generalstabes.* Berlin, 1931.

Foerster, Wolfgang. *Graf Schlieffen und der Weltkrieg.* Berlin, 1925.

Freytag-Loringhoven. *Heerfuehrung im Weltkriege.* Berlin, 1920.

Gatzke, Hans. *Germany's Drive to the West.* Baltimore, 1950.
Groener, William. *Lebenserinnerungen.* Goettingen, 1947.

Groener, William. "Die Liquidation des Weltkrieges," *Preussische Jahrbuecher.* Vol. 179. Berlin, 1920.

Groener, William. *Das Testament des Grafen Schlieffen.* Berlin, 1929.

Groener, William. *Der Feldherr wider Willen.* Berlin, 1931.

Groener, Dorothea. *General Groener.* Frankfurt/Main, 1955.

Hammann, Otto. *Zur Vorgeschichte des Weltkrieges.* Berlin, 1918.

Helfritz, Hans. Wilhelm II. Berlin, 1954.

Herzfeld, Hans. Die deutsche Ruestungspolitik vor dem Weltkriege. Leipzig, 1923.

Herzfeld, Hans. Die deutsche Sozialdemokratie und die Aufloesung der nationalen Einheitsfront im Weltkriege. Leipzig, 1928.

Heuss, Theodore. Friedrich Naumann. Berlin, 1937.

Huber, Ernst. Heer und Staat. Hamburg, 1938.

Hubatsch, Walther. Die Aera Tirpitz. Goettingen, 1955.

Kabisch, Ernst. Streitfragen des Weltkrieges 1914-1918. Stuttgart, 1924.

Kessel, Eberhard. Moltke. Stuttgart, 1957.

Kuhl, Hermann von. Der Weltkrieg 1914-1918. Berlin, 1935.

Kuhl, Hermann von. Der deutsche Generalstab. Berlin, 1920.

Meyer, Henry Cord. Mitteleuropa in German Thought and Action, 1815-1945. The Hague, 1955.

Meyer, Karl W. Karl Liebknecht. Washington, 1957.

Mommsen, Wolfgang J. Max Weber und die deutsche Politik. Tuebingen, 1959.

Montgelas, Max. Leitfaden zur Kriegsschuldfrage. Berlin, 1923.

Moser, Otto von. Ernsthafte Plaudereien ueber den Weltkrieg. Stuttgart, 1925.

Mueller-Loebnitz, Wilhelm. Die Sendung des Oberstleutnants Hentsch. Berlin, 1922.

Mueller, Richard. Vom Kaiserreich zur Republik. Vienna, 1924.

Naumann, Friedrich. Demokratie und Kaisertum. Berlin, 1904.

Niemann, Alfred. Revolution von Oben. Berlin, 1927.

Oncken, Hermann. Das alte und neue Europa. Gotha, 1917.

Prager, Eugen. Geschichte der Unabhaengige Sozial Demokratische Partei. Berlin, 1922.

Rapp, Adolf. Die Wuerttemberger und die nationale Frage 1863-1871. Stuttgart, 1907.

Reshetar, John S. The Ukrainian Revolution, 1917-1920. Princeton, 1952.

Ritter, Gerhard. Staatskunst und Kriegshandwerk. 2 vols. Munich, 1954-1960.

Ritter, Gerhard. Der Schlieffenplan. Munich, 1956.

Ritter, Gerhard. Lebendige Vergangenheit. Munich, 1958.

Ritter, Gerhard A. Die Arbeiterbewegung im Wilhelminischen Reich. Berlin, 1959.

Rosenberg, Arthur. The Birth of the German Republic. New York, 1931.

Rudin, Harry. Armistice 1918. Yale, 1944.

Sarter, Adolf. Die deutschen Eisenbahnen im Kriege. Berlin, 1930.

Scheel, Heinrich. Revolutionaere Ereignisse und Probleme in Deutschland. Berlin, 1957.

Schmidt-Bueckeberg, Rudolf. Das Militaerkabinett der preussischen Koenige und deutschen Kaiser. Berlin, 1933.

Schmoller, Gustav. Zwanzig Jahre Deutscher Politik. Leipzig, 1920.

Schorske, Carl E. German Social Democracy 1905-1917. Cambridge, 1955.

Schueddekopf, Otto-Ernst. Das Heer und die Republik. Frankfurt/Main, 1955.

Schwertfeger, Bernhard. Das Weltkriegsende. Potsdam, 1938.

Stadelmann, Rudolf. Deutschland und West Europa. Laupheim, 1948.

Stutzenberger, Adolf. <u>Die Abdankung Kaiser Wilhelms II.</u> Berlin, 1937.

Troeltsch, Ernst. <u>Spektator-Briefe.</u> Tuebingen, 1922.

Troeltsch, Ernst. <u>Deutscher Geist und Westeuropa.</u> Tuebingen, 1925.

Westarp, Kuno. <u>Das Ende der Monarchie.</u> Berlin, 1952.

Zmarzlik, Hans-Guenter. <u>Bethmann Hollweg als Reichs-kanzler 1909-1914.</u> Duesseldorf, 1957.

# INDEX